D1414026

# ECOLOGICAL ISSUES

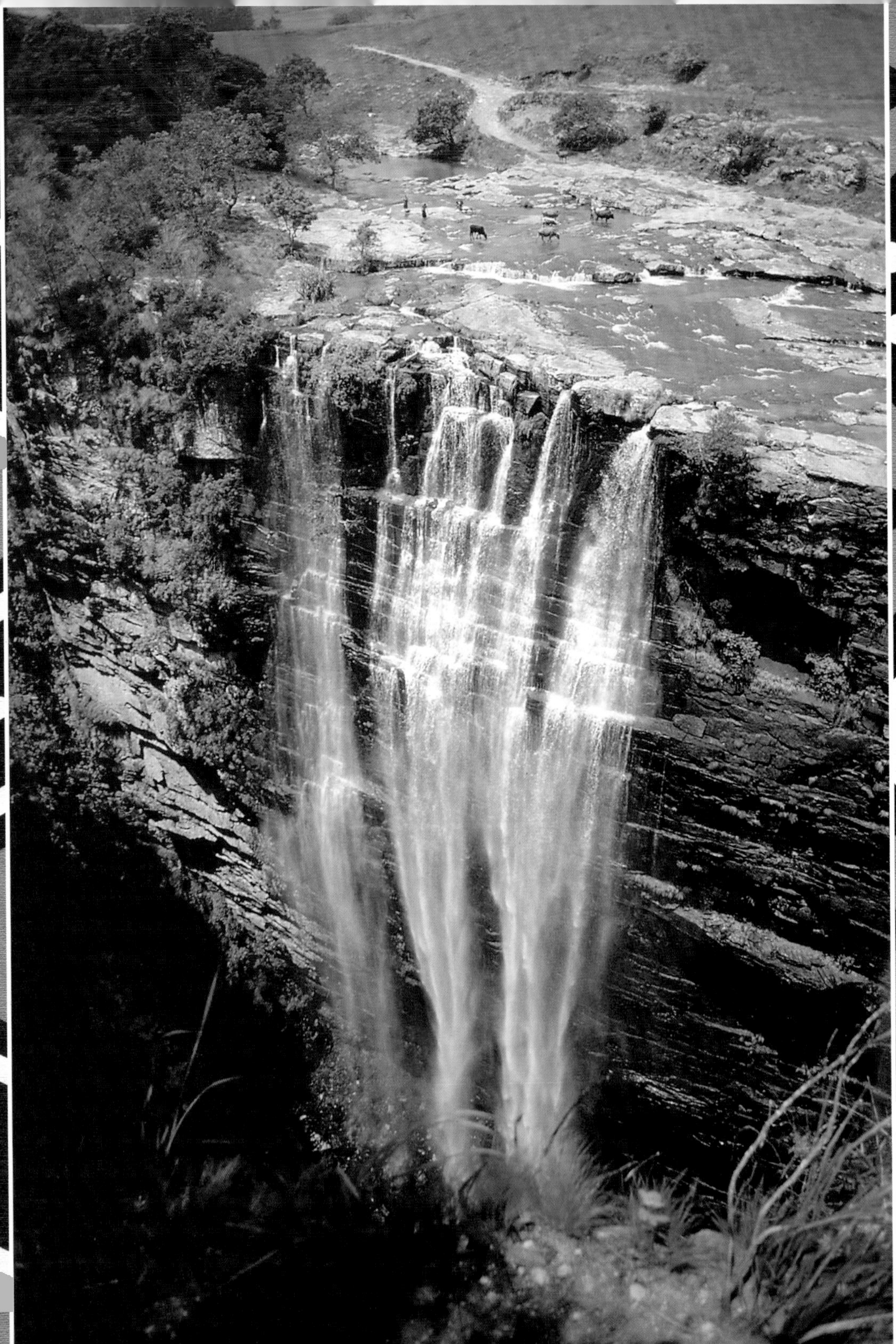

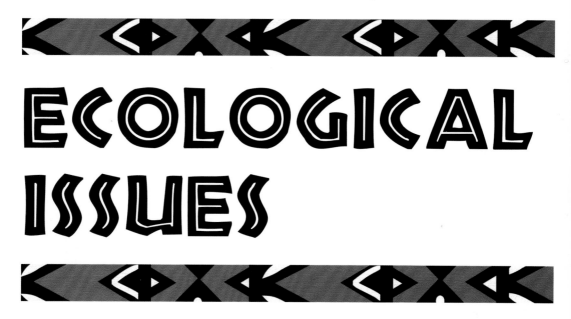

# ECOLOGICAL ISSUES

LeeAnne Gelletly

Mason Crest Publishers

Philadelphia

**Frontispiece: Magwa Falls, in South Africa's Eastern Cape Province.**

Produced by OTTN Publishing, Stockton, New Jersey

**Mason Crest Publishers**
370 Reed Road
Broomall, PA 19008
www.masoncrest.com

First printing

1 3 5 7 9 8 6 4 2


Library of Congress Cataloging-in-Publication Data

Gelletly, LeeAnne.
  Ecological issues in Africa / LeeAnne Gelletly.
     p. cm. — (Africa, progress and problems)
  Includes bibliographical references and index.
  ISBN-13: 978-1-59084-956-9 (hard cover)
  ISBN-10: 1-59084-956-6 (hard cover)
  1. Environmental conditions—Africa. 2. Environmental degradation—Africa. I. Title. II. Series.
  GE160.A35G45 2006
  333.72'096—dc22
                        2005016306

# TABLE OF CONTENTS

# AFRICA: PROGRESS & PROBLEMS

# THE PROMISE OF TODAY'S AFRICA

## by Robert I. Rotberg

Today's Africa is a mosaic of effective democracy and desperate despotism, immense wealth and abysmal poverty, conscious modernity and mired traditionalism, bitter conflict and vast arenas of peace, and enormous promise and abiding failure. Generalizations are more difficult to apply to Africa or Africans than elsewhere. The continent, especially the sub-Saharan two-thirds of its immense landmass, presents enormous physical, political, and human variety. From snow-capped peaks to intricate patches of remaining jungle, from desolate deserts to the greatest rivers, and from the highest coastal sand dunes anywhere to teeming urban conglomerations, Africa must be appreciated from myriad perspectives. Likewise, its peoples come in every shape and size, govern themselves in several complicated manners, worship a host of indigenous and imported gods, and speak thousands of original and five or six derivative common languages. To know Africa is to know nuance and complexity.

There are 53 nation-states that belong to the African Union, 48 of which are situated within the sub-Saharan mainland or on its offshore islands. No other continent has so many countries, political divisions, or members of the General Assembly of the United Nations. No other continent encompasses so many

distinctively different peoples or spans such geographical dis-
parity. On no other continent have so many innocent civilians
lost their lives in intractable civil wars—12 million since 1991
in such places as Algeria, Angola, the Congo, Côte d'Ivoire,
Liberia, Sierra Leone, and the Sudan. No other continent has so
many disparate natural resources (from cadmium, cobalt, and
copper to petroleum and zinc) and so little to show for their
frenzied exploitation. No other continent has proportionally so
many people subsisting (or trying to) on less than $1 a day. But
then no other continent has been so beset by HIV/AIDS (30
percent of all adults in southern Africa), by tuberculosis, by
malaria (prevalent almost everywhere), and by less well-known
scourges such as schistosomiasis (liver fluke), several kinds of
filariasis, river blindness, trachoma, and trypanosomiasis
(sleeping sickness).

Africa is the most Christian continent. It has more
Muslims than the Middle East. Apostolic and Pentecostal
churches are immensely powerful. So are Sufi brotherhoods.
Yet traditional African religions are still influential. So is a
belief in spirits and witches (even among Christians and
Muslims), in faith healing and in alternative medicine.
Polygamy remains popular. So does the practice of female cir-
cumcision and other long-standing cultural preferences.
Africa cannot be well understood without appreciating how
village life still permeates the great cities and how urban pursuits engulf villages. Half if not more of its peoples live in
towns and cities; no longer can Africa be considered predomi-
nantly rural, agricultural, or wild.

Political leaders must cater to both worlds, old and new. They and their followers must join the globalized, Internet-penetrated world even as they remain rooted appropriately in past modes of behavior, obedient to dictates of family, lineage, tribe, and ethnicity. This duality often results in democracy or at

least partially participatory democracy. Equally often it develops into autocracy. Botswana and Mauritius have enduring democratic governments. In Benin, Ghana, Kenya, Lesotho, Malawi, Mali, Mozambique, Namibia, Nigeria, Senegal, South Africa, Tanzania, and Zambia fully democratic pursuits are relatively recent and not yet sustainably implanted. Algeria, Cameroon, Chad, the Central African Republic, Egypt, the Sudan, and Tunisia are authoritarian entities run by strongmen. Zimbabweans and Equatorial Guineans suffer from even more venal rule. Swazis and Moroccans are subject to the real whims of monarchs. Within even this vast sweep of political practice there are still more distinctions. The partial democracies represent a spectrum. So does the manner in which authority is wielded by kings, by generals, and by long-entrenched civilian autocrats.

The democratic countries are by and large better developed and more rapidly growing economically than those ruled by strongmen. In Africa there is an association between the pursuit of good governance and beneficial economic performance. Likewise, the natural resource wealth curse that has afflicted mineral-rich countries such as the Congo and Nigeria has had the opposite effect in well-governed places like Botswana. Nation-states open to global trade have done better than those with closed economies. So have those countries with prudent managements, sensible fiscal arrangements, and modest deficits. Overall, however, the bulk of African countries have suffered in terms of reduced economic growth from the sheer fact of being tropical, beset by disease in an enervating climate

where there is an average of one trained physician to every 13,000 persons. Many lose growth prospects, too, because of the absence of navigable rivers, the paucity of ocean and river ports, barely maintained roads, and few and narrow railroads. Moreover, 15 of Africa's countries are landlocked, without comfortable access to relatively inexpensive waterborne transport. Hence, imports and exports for much of Africa are more expensive than elsewhere as they move over formidable distances. Africa is the most underdeveloped continent because of geographical and health constraints that have not yet been overcome, because of ill-considered policies, because of the sheer number of separate nation-states (a colonial legacy), and because of poor governance.

Africa's promise is immense, and far more exciting than its achievements have been since a wave of nationalism and independence in the 1960s liberated nearly every section of the continent. Thus, the next several decades of the 21st century are ones of promise for Africa. The challenges are clear: to alleviate grinding poverty and deliver greater real economic goods to larger proportions of people in each country, and across all 53 countries; to deliver more of the benefits of good governance to more of Africa's peoples; to end the destructive killing fields that run rampant across so much of Africa; to improve educational training and health services; and to roll back the scourges of HIV/AIDS, tuberculosis, and malaria. Every challenge represents an opportunity with concerted and bountiful Western assistance to transform the lives of Africa's vulnerable and resourceful future generations.

# 1 AFRICA AND ITS ENVIRONMENT: AN OVERVIEW

The world's second-largest continent, Africa boasts a remarkably varied environment. It is a land of huge arid deserts, moist tropical rainforests, vast grassy savannas, and snowcapped mountains. Inhabiting the land are thousands of species of mammals, reptiles, amphibians, birds, insects, and marine life, reflecting a rich biodiversity. Yet the 53 independent countries (including island nations) that make up Africa face a multitude of environmental issues, many of which threaten the future of the people who live on this vast continent.

## MOUNTAINS AND DESERTS

Covering approximately 11,657,000 square miles (30,190,000 square kilometers), Africa makes up around one-fifth of the earth's total land area. The continent can be divided into three major regions: the northern plateau, central and southern plateau, and eastern highlands.

Africa's northern plateau and its central and southern plateau consist mainly of lowlands ranging from 500 to 2,000 feet (150 to 610 meters) above sea level. Elevations are somewhat higher in the northwest corner of the continent, where the plateau is broken up by the Atlas mountain range, which extends more than 1,200 miles (1,930 km) through Morocco, Algeria, and Tunisia.

Much greater heights can be found in Africa's eastern highlands, which extend south from the Red Sea. There, elevations average more than 5,000 feet (1,500 meters) above sea level. East Africa contains the continent's two largest mountain peaks: Kilimanjaro, which rises 19,331 feet (5,892 meters) in northern Tanzania, along the border with Kenya; and Mount Kenya,

**Kilimanjaro, Africa's highest mountain, actually consists of three separate volcanoes: Kibo, Mawenzi, and Shira. It is located in northern Tanzania.**

which soars to 17,058 feet (5,199 meters) in central Kenya. A unique feature of the eastern highlands is the Great Rift Valley— a vast geologic fault system made up of deep, steep valleys.

The northern part of Africa lays claim to the world's largest desert, the Sahara, which extends 3,500 miles (5,630 km) from west to east across much of the continent's northern plateau. Covering some 3.5 million square miles (9 million sq km), the Sahara includes parts of Mauritania, Mali, Niger, Chad, Sudan, Egypt, Libya, Tunisia, Algeria, Morocco, and Western Sahara. Two other major deserts of Africa lie to the south: In the far southwestern part of Africa is the Namib Desert, which stretches along the Atlantic coast. The Kalahari Desert covers parts of Namibia and South Africa, and much of Botswana.

Oases dot these hot, arid desert lands, providing places of nourishment for the native trees, which include date palms, tamarisks, and acacias. Among the scattered desert wildlife are the ostrich, gazelle, antelope, jackal, and hyena.

# RAINFORESTS AND SAVANNAS

Within the west-central region of Africa lies the Congo rainforest, the second-largest rainforest of the world (smaller only than the Amazon rainforest of South America). Encompassing land fed by the Congo River and its tributaries, the rainforest lies in the center of Africa and covers as much as 500 million acres (202 million hectares).

This immense forest hosts an amazing biodiversity, with plant and animal species numbering in the millions. As many as 100 different kinds of trees can be found within 1 square mile (2.6 sq km) of land. They commonly include oil palms; fruit trees; ebony, mahogany, and other hardwoods; and softwoods such as okoume. Among the Congo rainforest's countless plants and animals are endangered species such as the mountain gorilla, the bonobo (pygmy chimpanzee), and the okapi (related to the giraffe). Many small mammals, along with hundreds of species of birds, live in the canopy.

Other, smaller rainforests grow in parts of western Africa and in Madagascar, a large island nation off the continent's southeastern coast. Woodlands containing mostly olive and oak trees can be found in the northwestern parts of Africa and in parts of the south. Forests of mangrove trees stretch stilt-like roots into the salty waters along Africa's eastern and western coasts.

Grassland plains, called savannas, cover large expanses of Africa. These areas feature tall grasses, thorny euphorbia bushes, and scattered baobab and acacia trees. Covering about two-fifths of the continent, Africa's savanna plains extend across eastern Africa, just south of the Sahara, and then curve around the Congo rainforest westward toward the Atlantic Ocean.

Within these immense plains, millions of antelope (including waterbuck, bushbuck, springbok, oryx, and impala), buffalo, giraffes, zebras, and wildebeest migrate in search of food and water. Many of them frequent the grasslands of Tanzania's Serengeti and Kenya's Masai Mara each year, feeding on their lush pastures. Some fall victim to predators such as cheetahs, hyenas, leopards, and lions, which also make the savanna their home. Africa's elephants live in both savannas and forests, with the largest numbers in the savannas of central, eastern, and southern Africa.

Northeastern Africa lays claim to the world's longest river, the Nile, which flows 4,160 miles (6,695 km) northward from east-central Africa to the Mediterranean Sea. Other major rivers of Africa include the Congo and Niger, which empty into the Atlantic Ocean, and the Zambezi, which flows into the Indian Ocean. In its course to the east, the Zambezi produces an impressive waterfall and popular tourist attraction, Victoria Falls, which is located between Zambia and Zimbabwe. Crocodiles and hippopotamuses can be found in many of the tropical rivers and swamps of Africa.

# PRESSURES ON THE ENVIRONMENT

Although Africa is famous for its unique wildlife and other natural attractions, the continent is also known for having some of the poorest countries in the world. Poverty and dramatic population increases (the number of people living in Africa rose from 364 million in 1970 to more than 800 million by the beginning of the 21st century) have created or exacerbated environmental stresses.

Although Africa's desert and forest regions remain sparsely populated, its river basins have attracted large numbers of people. The areas of Africa with the greatest population densities include the Niger River Basin (Nigeria), the Nile River Basin (including Egypt and Sudan), and the Great Lakes region, which includes the countries of Burundi, Rwanda, Uganda, Kenya, and Tanzania. These East African countries surround the lakes of Kivu, Tanganyika, and Victoria. Africa's two largest cities are in North Africa (Cairo, Egypt) and West Africa (Lagos, Nigeria).

Although Africa's natural resources are many, most of the continent's countries are poor. In fact, they are classified as developing nations (countries with low per capita income, where many impoverished citizens grow just enough food for themselves and their families to survive). About half of the 600 million people living in sub-Saharan Africa (the region south of the Sahara Desert) live on the equivalent of 65 cents a day.

Many of Africa's poor survive by subsistence farming; others work as traditional pastoralists, migrating with their herds of cattle, sheep, and goats in search of pastureland. Still others who are hungry turn to hunting wild animals illegally, or poaching.

Intensive farming practices and overgrazing have degraded much of Africa's land, while hunting has decimated wildlife populations.

However, African societies are becoming less agrarian and more industrialized. By the year 2000, nearly 40 percent of Africa's people were living in urban areas, according to the United Nations Centre for Settlements–Habitat. While other

At the turn of the 20th century, only 5 percent of Africa's population lived in cities and towns. Today that figure stands at about 40 percent—and is rising rapidly. This photo was taken in the West African country of Liberia.

regions of the world—such as North America, South America, and Europe—had significantly higher overall rates of urbanization, the proportion of the population living in cities was increasing fastest in Africa. Since the mid-1990s, growing numbers of African villagers have migrated to cities in search of jobs. This influx of new residents has strained—and in some cases overwhelmed—the infrastructure of cities and caused serious environmental problems, including air, land, and water pollution.

Although Africa's people depend heavily on the land for their survival, the continent's natural resources are shrinking rapidly from overuse and overharvesting. The pressures of poverty make conservation difficult, as people engaged in a daily struggle to survive are naturally less inclined to focus on long-term issues. In many cases, Africans are using up the continent's renewable resources (resources that can be replaced with time through natural processes) at a faster pace than these resources can be replenished.

# NEED FOR SUSTAINABILITY

The solution to Africa's environmental problems, according to some conservationists, is to emphasize the sustainable use of resources—that is, to prevent resources from being degraded or lost faster than they are regenerated (as occurs with the overharvesting of trees, the killing of endangered species, or the degradation of land through overfarming or pollution).

In struggling to address environmental issues affecting the entire world, many countries and international organizations have reached similar conclusions. In 1987 the United Nations (UN) introduced the idea of sustainable development. In a report called "Our Common Future," *sustainable use* was defined as "meeting the needs of the present without compromising the ability of future generations to meet their own needs." According to the report, by developing sustainable practices the world's nations could ensure the survival and well-being of the entire earth.

Discussions on the environmental issues raised by the 1987 report took place at a United Nations Conference for Environment and Development, held in Rio de Janeiro, Brazil, in 1992. Dubbed the Earth Summit, this gathering was attended by representatives of 172 nations, including many from Africa. By the end of the conference, a number of international initiatives and agreements had been established to address environmental issues such as biological diversity, the preservation of forests, and environmentally sustainable development. UN organizations and programs that address many of the issues resulting from the Earth Summit include the Commission on Sustainable Development, the United Nations Environment Program (UNEP), and the United Nations Development Program (UNDP).

# A CONTINENT AT RISK

In July 2002 the UNEP, based in Nairobi, Kenya, called on African leaders to govern their countries in "environmentally friendly" ways. The UNEP report noted that the many nations within Africa face a multitude of environmental problems that threaten to increase poverty and bring much of the continent's wildlife to extinction. Among the most significant issues, the report noted, were the continuing loss of wildlife and animal habitat, a dramatic increase in air and water pollution, and climate change.

In Africa deforestation (the clearing of forests) and desertification (the process by which viable land is turned into desert land) have destroyed animal habitats. Uncontrolled hunting and the illegal trade in wildlife have caused a dramatic decline in Africa's biodiversity. Air, water, and land pollution have caused illnesses and diseases that sicken and kill millions of Africans each year. Climate change attributed to global warming has been blamed for worsening droughts and water shortages in some areas, and floods in others.

Clearly, however, Africa must confront the issue of poverty if it is ever to adequately address environmental concerns over the use of its natural resources. Actions taken to improve the low standard of living of the poor (for example, increasing access to agricultural technology, clean water and sanitation, and electricity) will directly benefit the continent's environment.

By 2050, according to UN estimates, Africa will be home to an additional billion people. The future of the continent depends on balancing the needs of its people with the conservation of its environment.

# DEFORESTATION

One of the most pressing environmental problems in Africa is deforestation. According to some estimates, more than three-quarters of the forest cover in many sub-Saharan nations has been lost. Eastern and western Africa retain only 7 percent and 14 percent, respectively, of their original forest cover. According to a 2003 report by the Food and Agricultural Organization of the United Nations, Africa's forest cover declined by 0.8 percent each year between 1990 and 2000.

## CUTTING OF TREES FOR FUELWOOD

Much of the African forests have been cut down because of the need for wood to heat homes and, especially, to fuel cooking fires. Fuelwood is an important source of energy for the people living in sub-Saharan Africa, where about 75 percent of cut wood is used for household cooking.

Not surprisingly, the highest rates of deforestation are occurring in areas with rapidly

(Opposite) A group of men in Guinea walk through a tree nursery. Guinea, like other nations in sub-Saharan Africa, has been losing forest cover at an alarming rate in recent years.

growing populations. One of the most severely affected areas is the Sudano-Sahel, a dry grassland region located south of the Sahara that encompasses all or parts of 12 African nations (including Ethiopia, Senegal, Mauritania, Mali, Niger, Nigeria, Chad, and Sudan). At the rate that fuelwood is being cut, it is estimated that by 2025 many parts of Africa will have lost their forests, resulting in serious shortages of this energy source.

## CLEARING LAND FOR CROPS AND LIVESTOCK

Huge swaths of the continent's forests have already been lost to agriculture, cleared and converted to cropland or pastureland for livestock. In Africa, farmers often clear land using a tradi-tional practice known as "slash and burn"—trees are cut down and the grasslands burned to make way for planting crops. Sometimes these managed fires rage out of control, consuming not only forests but farm-land as well. The fires can also cause chemical changes to the soil, reduc-ing its fertility.

Slash-and-burn agriculture has cost the country of Ethiopia more for-est cover than most other African nations. Within the past 40 years, Ethiopia's forest cover has been reduced from 40 percent of the land to only 2.7 percent. A report com-piled for the UN Emergencies Unit for Ethiopia estimates that at this rate of deforestation, the nation will have no natural forests by 2020.

Environmentalists recommend that countries should have a minimum of 10 percent forest cover. However, Ethiopia is not the only African nation with significantly less than the minimum. Kenya has also lost most of its forests, which now cover just 1.7 percent of the land.

Slash-and-burn farming has also decimated wide sections of the tropical rainforests of Madagascar, the large island nation off the coast of southeastern Africa. Famed for its huge variety of unusual plants and animals, Madagascar contains 200,000 different species. Three-quarters of these are endemic species (found naturally nowhere else in the world), such as the long-tailed, monkeylike lemurs, which make their home in the island's rainforests. Over the years, farmers growing rice and other crops have eked out a living on Madagascar by clearing land at the expense of rainforest habitat. Some researchers estimate that just 15 percent of Madagascar's original forest cover remains today.

The ring-tailed lemur, one of Madagascar's unique species, is threatened by destruction of the island's rainforests.

## COMMERCIAL LOGGING

Forests are also being cut down by logging companies. Many African nations have found that the timber industry can add significant revenue to their economy. In Cameroon, for example, tropical timber products make up about 20 percent of the country's export income. However, the country is undergoing one of the greatest rates of forest loss in the world. In nearby Côte d'Ivoire, most of the forests (once the largest in West Africa) are gone because of uncontrolled logging.

One of the most heavily logged regions of Africa is the Congo Basin, home to the world's second-largest rainforest. Valuable tropical woods found here include hardwoods such as ebony, mahogany, and sipo, used to make musical instruments, furniture, veneers, and other wood products. An important softwood is okoume, which is used to make plywood and flooring.

At least 10 African nations lay claim to parts of the Congo rainforest, a vast region that covers an area three times larger than the state of California. Most of these countries have made agreements, or concessions, with commercial logging companies looking to take advantage of the growing international demand for tropical timber. In 2004 the International Tropical Timber Organization (ITTO), which encourages sustainable forestry, published a study of logging practices in Cameroon, the Central African Republic, the Democratic Republic of the Congo, Gabon, Guinea, and the Republic of the Congo. The report noted that while Congo logging companies harvested about 35 tree species, the bulk of the harvest consisted of only the 6 most valuable species, such as the gaboon mahogany and sapele mahogany. Because of the cost of transporting timber to market, logging companies tended to cut only those trees with the greatest value on the tropical timber market.

Although Congo Basin governments usually include restrictions when they award logging concessions, individuals and companies often ignore the rules and bribe officials who are supposed to monitor their cutting activities. For example, logging in Cameroon was supposed to be restricted to 6,200 acres (2,500 hectares) per year. But some logging companies with agreements valid for 33 years emptied the forests of their valuable tropical hardwood within just three years.

Timber—particularly tropical hardwoods such as ebony, mahogany, and sipo—is a major source of income for African nations in the Congo Basin. But uncontrolled logging threatens this valuable resource. In fact, at current rates of exploitation, experts predict that the Congo rainforest will be completely gone by 2020.

Even when logging companies abide by the agreements limiting their harvests, that is no guarantee that forests will not be overcut. Once previously undisturbed forests have been opened up for legal logging with the establishment of trails and roads, illegal logging often follows.

In its 2004 study the ITTO also reported that Congo Basin governments had granted logging rights to about 40 percent of rainforest that up until then had remained undisturbed. According to some estimates, the Congo rainforests are being destroyed at rate of 10 million acres (4 million hectares) per year. Researchers have predicted that unless this rate of destruction is reduced, the rainforest will be gone by 2020.

# IMPACT OF FOREST LOSS

Forests affect the quality of water, soil, and air. As water filters through tree roots and soil, it is naturally filtered and cleaned. Trees and their undergrowth also help keep the soil soft and porous, which allows the ground to absorb large amounts of water. This absorbed water seeps through the soil on the way to underground reservoirs, or aquifers, which ultimately feed rivers, streams, and wells. When forests are cleared, water that would have fed underground rivers and streams is instead lost to evaporation.

Forests also prevent soil erosion. When trees are cut down, soil becomes less porous and able to absorb water. During heavy

The Ba'aka people, who are indigenous to the Congo rainforest, find their traditional way of life increasingly under threat from logging. Not only does the unsustainable harvesting of timber destroy habitat for the animals that the Ba'aka hunt, but contact with loggers and proximity to logging towns has left the Ba'aka vulnerable to unscrupulous outsiders who seek to exploit their unfamiliarity with modern life.

rainstorms, water will flow over the hardened ground surface of deforested land, carrying dirt and other sediment to nearby streams. This runoff pollutes waterways and, in some cases, results in flooding.

Even the atmosphere is affected by the presence of forests. Trees absorb carbon dioxide and give off oxygen as they grow, in a process called photosynthesis. The loss of large swaths of forest results in a reduction in the amount of oxygen emitted into the air, as well as an increase in the amount of carbon dioxide in the atmosphere. Rainforests, in particular, are considered essential for absorbing carbon dioxide.

Forest loss also means habitat loss for many living creatures. Rainforests are particularly valued for their biodiversity. Humans also depend on these rainforests. Nearly 20 million people who live in and around the Congo rainforest use its resources for food, fuel, and shelter. Among them are the Ba'aka, the indigenous people of the Congo forests. Their traditional way of life, based on sustainable hunting of wildlife and gathering of native plants, is threatened as the Congo rainforest disappears.

## RESPONSIBLE LOGGING

Although logging brings jobs—it employs 3 to 8 percent of the workforce in the Congo Basin—once the trees are gone, so are the jobs. Uncontrolled logging in West Africa has already resulted in the loss of 90 percent of the original rainforest. This land was never converted to agricultural use. Instead, it was abandoned, leaving the local people even more impoverished because of the loss of their forests.

Good timber management requires a balance between harvesting wood and allowing time for regrowth. Such "sustained yield" timber management ensures a continuous supply of trees. However, sustainable management is seldom practiced in African forests.

# PROTECTING THE RAINFOREST

At the World Summit on Sustainable Development, held in Johannesburg, South Africa, in September 2002, the United States and other countries joined with the governments of Cameroon, the Central African Republic, the Democratic Republic of the Congo, Equatorial Guinea, Gabon, and the Republic of the Congo to form the Congo Basin Forest Partnership. This government initiative promised to set aside 29 forest areas as protected reserves and 11 other regions as sites in which responsible forestry practices and natural resource conservation would take place.

The agreement protects about 40 percent of the Congo Basin within a network of new national parks and previously established preserves. The initiative also calls on nations to make responsible forestry logging agreements and to assist communities that depend on forest resources. The United States promised a grant of $53 million to help fund the project through 2005.

Critics noted that the indigenous people of the rainforest, the Ba'aka, were not involved with the initiation of the program or even informed of park development plans. Many observers believed it unfair to set aside land for forest preserves without the input or agreement of those who live in and depend upon the forests.

# SUSTAINABLE FORESTRY

An international private conservation organization called the WWF (formerly known as the World Wildlife Fund) has been working for many years to persuade Congo Basin governments to better regulate logging in the region. In 1999 the group sponsored a "forest summit" in Yaounde, the capital of Cameroon. At that time, five central African countries agreed to set aside areas of forest for protection. They also agreed to work toward sustainable forest management.

By the time of the second forest summit—held in Brazzaville, Republic of the Congo, in February 2005—seven African nations (the Republic of the Congo, Gabon, São Tomé and Príncipe, Equatorial Guinea, Congo, Chad, and the Central African Republic) were willing to commit to protecting the rainforest. Their leaders signed a joint treaty pledging the seven nations to work together to combat poachers and to provide funds for training security staff and park rangers. To better protect the Congo rainforest from uncontrolled logging, the treaty also called for the establishment of uniform logging laws in the seven participating countries.

Another part of the agreement expressed the intent to create a certification system for the tropical woods being logged from the region. Such a system would allow purchasers in Western markets to know where the wood originated and to be assured that it had been logged in a sustainable manner.

Among those attending the 2005 forest summit in Brazzaville was Kenya's deputy environmental minister, Wangari Maathai. In the late 1970s Maathai had founded the Greenbelt Movement, which worked to restore deforest-

Kenya's Wangari Maathai won the 2004 Nobel Peace Prize for her Greenbelt Movement, which teaches women how to plant and care for tree seedlings, producing economic as well as environmental benefits. She was the first African woman to receive the award.

ed land in her native Kenya. In the three decades since its establishment, the movement has spread across Africa: about 10,000 rural women have received training in how to plant and care for seedlings of indigenous trees such as acacia, cedar, and baobab. In all, the reforestation movement has been responsible for the planting of some 30 million trees throughout Africa.

Maathai founded the Greenbelt Movement as a way to improve Kenya's degraded land. However, the program has also served to improve economic prospects in impoverished rural areas and empower women. Maathai's activities brought her into conflict with the country's government, for she saw that corruption was to blame for many of Kenya's environmental problems. Although persecuted for years for her activism, Maathai ultimately became Kenya's deputy environmental minister under a friendlier administration. In 2004 she became the first African woman and the first environmentalist to win the Nobel Peace Prize.

# SOIL DEGRADATION AND DESERTIFICATION

esertification refers to the degradation of healthy, productive soil so that it can no longer support plant life. Land degradation occurs when topsoil is lost to erosion or has its nutrients depleted. Desertification is caused by human activities, such as deforestation, overcultivation, overgrazing, or poor irrigation practices.

Africa, which is about two-thirds desert and dryland, has been particularly vulnerable to desertification. According to the UN, almost three-quarters of agricultural dryland in Africa has already been degraded to some degree.

## LAND DEGRADATION FROM DEFORESTATION

In Africa, desertification is occurring in areas where forests are being cleared for use as fuel or to make room for agriculture. The removal of vegetation reduces the ability of the land to hold water and increases topsoil erosion. As the earth dries out, the land loses its ability to support plant life.

(Opposite) The barren land in Mali where this woman walks is part of the Sahel, the semiarid region between the Sahara Desert to the north and the wet regions to the south. Because of overgrazing and poor irrigation techniques in the Sahel, much of the arable land there is being lost to the encroaching desert.

One of the regions most seriously affected by desertification is the Sahel. A heavily populated area, the Sahel consists of grassy drylands that lie south of the Sahara and extend through large parts of Senegal, Mauritania, Mali, Burkina Faso, Niger, Nigeria, Chad, and Sudan. Certain arid regions in Eritrea, Ethiopia, Kenya, and Somalia are also considered part of the Sahel. The name, which is Arabic for "border," refers to the region of land that serves as a transition zone between the Sahara Desert to the north and the tropical areas to the south.

The Sahel environment consists mostly of savanna vegetation such as drought-resistant grasses and shrubs. Scattered trees used to be found throughout the landscape, but since the 1970s, researchers say, about 30 percent of them have been cut down.

# OVERLY INTENSIVE AGRICULTURAL USE

Only about 8 percent of the land of Africa is arable, or suitable for farming. Most other land has topsoil that is very thin and low

in nutrients, so agricultural plots typically produce good crop yields for only a few years.

In Africa the soil tends to lose its nutrients fairly quickly because farmers traditionally practice "shifting cultivation," which involves planting the same crops year after year. After several years, when the soil's nutrients have been exhausted, the farmer moves on to a new location, and the abandoned plot is allowed to return to grass and regain soil fertility. However, in times of prolonged drought, it seldom does.

In many cases, when it is not possible to move on to new land, the very poor have no choice but to keep using the same plot. They overuse the land to the point where it can no longer support any plant growth at all.

Such desertification of the land is a problem in the Sahel and in the Kenyan and Ethiopian highlands of eastern Africa. In Ethiopia, which has been farmed for more than 7,000 years, the soil has been severely eroding because of continuous plantings of nutrient-draining crops such as coffee (a major export) and teff (a native grain found only in that region). More than 50 percent of the land in Kenya has been abandoned because of soil degradation.

Land degradation also occurs from livestock overgrazing. Many people of the Sahel and eastern highlands—such as the Dinka, the Fulani, the Maasai, and the Somali—practice nomadic herding. They travel with cattle, sheep, goats, and camels to various pasturelands in search of food and water. Sometimes, these livestock herds destroy so much vegetation that subsequent rains cause severe water runoff and soil erosion. Surface runoff also can occur when herds trample soil so much that it becomes compacted.

# POOR IRRIGATION PRACTICES

Badly managed or excessive irrigation can also wreak devastation on farmland. When too much water stands in fields that have poor drainage, salt builds up in the soil as the water evapo-rates. This accumulation of salt in the soil, or salinization, severely reduces the land's ability to sustain plant growth.

Taking too much water from rivers and lakes for irrigation purposes can also dry up the land. A dramatic example of the effects of overly intensive irrigation is the Sahel's Lake Chad. The lake, which straddles the borders of Chad, Niger, Nigeria, and Cameroon, was once one of Africa's largest bodies of water, but drought and loss of water due to heavy irrigation have shrunk it from 9,700 square miles (25,000 sq km) in 1963 to around 520 square miles (1,350 sq km) by the turn of the 21st century.

(Right) Lake Chad used to cover the entire area within the blue line, but it had shrunk to the part within the red line by 2002, when this satellite photo was taken. The shiny, rippled sections above and to the left are sand dunes, not water. (Below) An irrigation canal built in Nigeria to carry water from Lake Chad is little more than a puddle.

During a severe drought in the 1960s, local farmers began to divert water from the shallow lake and its two major tributaries, the Chari and Logone Rivers. By the early 1980s, the amount of water being withdrawn had quadrupled as less rain fell and cropland required even more irrigation.

At the same time, intense grazing of the surrounding savanna was depleting its vegetation. This continuing loss of grasses and plant life caused the land to continue to dry out. And as less moisture was being recycled back into the atmosphere from the drying earth, even less rainfall was seen. The result is a severely shrunken Lake Chad, which can no longer support the 9 million farmers, fishermen, and herders in the region who had depended on it for water, food, and their livelihoods.

Desertification throughout the Sahel region continues to be a severe environmental problem. Some scientists estimate that the Sahara Desert is spreading along parts of its southern edge by up to 30 miles (48 km) a year.

# EFFECTS OF DESERTIFICATION

Desertification makes land prone to floods and can cause soils to build up salt deposits. Once soil has been depleted of nutrients and eroded, it is more likely to be blown away by the wind or washed away during heavy rains. Strong winds carrying eroded soil become dust storms, which sometimes travel hundreds or even thousands of miles, sandblasting homes and machinery, killing vegetation, and causing health problems such as eye infections, respiratory disease, and allergies.

As the land's fertility decreases, farmers experience crop failures and lose their livestock. As food production declines, the region's inhabitants often face malnutrition and starvation. Drought and desertification have been blamed for causing a great famine that occurred in the Sahel from 1968 to 1974. At that time more than 200,000 people died and millions of animals perished.

Desertification often drives massive numbers of people from their homes in search of food and water. Frequently they migrate to cities and camps, where their vast numbers can cause additional pressures on the environment. Disputes over water and scarce grazing lands have led to political instability, civil unrest, and even armed conflict, loss of life, and forced migrations. The UN Convention to Combat Desertification estimates that in the next 20 years, some 60 million people will move from devastated areas of sub-Saharan Africa toward northern Africa and Europe.

# REHABILITATING DEGRADED LANDS

One way to prevent desertification is to encourage farmers to rotate crops and to raise plants that replace lost nutrients, such as nitrogen, in the soil. Legumes such as soybeans will restore nitrogen, while cereal grains such as corn or wheat deplete this nutrient.

In Kenya, which has seen severe soil degradation, a program is under way to dissuade farmers from planting their usual crops of corn, millet, and beans. Yields from these crops have been declining for several years as the soil has eroded. The World Agroforestry Centre, formerly called the International Council for Research in Agroforestry and still referred to by the acronym ICRAF, is promoting alternative tree-based businesses, such as orchards or fodder tree plantations. The ICRAF maintains that planting trees rehabilitates soil by adding organic matter to it and breaks up the crust, or "hard pan," that forms on the surface of degraded earth.

The ICRAF has also been working with farmers in Kenya, Malawi, Mozambique, Tanzania, Zambia, and Zimbabwe, promoting the use of "fertilizer trees" to rehabilitate degraded land. These tree species can actually transfer nitrogen from the air into the soil. Farmers who have planted the fertilizer trees in their grain fields have reported improved soil quality and crop yields as much as four times higher than those reported at neighboring farms—without the use of mineral fertilizers. Although the farmland in these countries has been depleted of nutrients from repeated plantings of corn, the fertilizer trees appear to be revitalizing the land.

About 100,000 farmers have participated in the ICRAF program, using fertilizer tree species such as the *Gliricidia sepium*. This tree has been shown to transform severely degraded land to productive farmland within two years of planting, and it grows well in the sandy soils and dry conditions of southern Africa. Even when severely cut back, its root system will still produce nitrogen. And its leaves can be used as a rich fertilizer as well.

An additional benefit of fertilizer trees is that once established, some species (such as the *Sesbania*) can be cut back each year for fuelwood. This could help alleviate the stress being placed on southern Africa's woodlands, which are being rapidly depleted for fuelwood.

Another green technology that can prevent soil degradation is the planting of "live fences." These barriers consist of trees or shrubs that are planted either fairly close together in a line or far enough apart to serve as fence posts for barbed wire. Such barriers are useful in controlling the movement of

The World Agroforestry Centre promotes the planting of *Gliricidia sepium* trees. In addition to restoring depleted soil, this species is a natural insect repellent. Farmers bathe their animals in a paste made from the leaves in order to keep disease-ridden pests away.

livestock, and they can also serve as windbreaks to prevent soil erosion.

# UN CONVENTION TO COMBAT DESERTIFICATION

Desertification was one of the many environmental issues addressed at the 1992 Rio Earth Summit. More than 180 countries have signed on to the United Nations Convention to Combat Desertification (UNCCD), which entered into force in December 1996. All 47 countries of sub-Saharan Africa belong to the UNCCD, which is funded through the Global Environment Facility, an independent financial organization.

Recognizing the importance of convincing local people to change practices that contribute to desertification, the UNCCD supports various educational and preventive programs. Such efforts include the planting of drought-resistant shrubs as barriers against advancing sand dunes, the planting of hardy crops and trees, and the promotion of alternative sources of energy (including solar and wind energy) so that trees will not be cut down for fuelwood.

Many such anti-desertification projects strive to directly

Hama Arba Diallo, executive secretary of the United Nations Convention to Combat Desertification, speaks at the group's 2003 conference in Havana, Cuba. Education programs form a large part of the UNCCD's strategy to protect land that is at risk of desertification.

involve the people most affected—those who live in areas identified as susceptible to desertification. For example, in Shantumbu, Zambia, the Zambia Alliance of Women took charge of educating the people in their community about energy-efficient and environmentally friendly cooking stoves. In so doing, the group helped prevent local forest areas from being chopped down for fuelwood.

In northern Ghana, villagers in Wulugu made a commitment to grow a forest. With the help of Friends of the Earth–Ghana and the Japan Fund for Global Environment, they planted about 2,000 acacia saplings on 13 acres (5.2 hectares) of land, with the plan to harvest the trees later, as needed, for home use and for sale.

# THREATS TO AFRICA'S WILDLIFE AND NATIVE PLANTS

The vast African continent is home to a stunning variety of animals and plants. But in recent decades serious threats to this biodiversity—including loss of habitat, overhunting, and the wildlife trade—have emerged. Today many species native to Africa are classified as endangered.

## ENDANGERED SPECIES

The World Conservation Union (also known as the International Union for the Conservation of Nature and Natural Resources, or IUCN) has categorized thousands of plant and animal species from around the world as endangered. Those species that are threatened or in danger of dying off altogether have been listed in the IUCN's "Red List of Threatened Species," which contains many of Africa's native plants and animals.

Among the endangered species native to Africa are antelopes such as the Dama gazelle and western giant eland; large cats such as the cheetah and leopard; primates such as the mandrill, chimpanzee, bongo, and mountain gorilla; and the black rhinoceros and white rhinoceros. Endangered plants include the leopard orchid and king protea (the national flower of South Africa).

## HABITAT LOSS

Deforestation and desertification have caused the destruction of many of the ecosystems in Africa. Defined as the interrelated network of living and nonliving things in a particular area, an ecosystem has specific characteristics (air, water, soil, and other species) that the creatures living there need to survive.

A mountain gorilla in the Democratic Republic of the Congo's Kahuzi Biega National Park. Deforestation and poaching have pushed the mountain gorilla, the largest of the apes, to the brink of extinction.

For example, the ecosystem of the African savanna consists of poor soil, low rainfall (with a wet and dry season), and a hot climate. Plants that have adapted to the savanna habitat include low trees and shrubs, as well as tall, drought-resistant grasses. Much savanna wildlife consists of large mammals and migratory birds that instinctively know when and where they must travel to find food and water.

But desertification has affected the savanna habitat in many areas, resulting in dried-up vegetation and water holes. Further savanna-habitat loss has occurred as people compete with wildlife for access to water and convert wilderness into farms and pastureland. Loss of savanna habitat has contributed to the dwindling numbers of the savanna elephant, lion, cheetah, and black rhinoceros.

Similarly, the rainforest habitat has also been affected by human presence. People have cut and burned down forests to clear land for development and for farms. Villages and settlements have isolated and surrounded populations of great apes and forest elephants. Logging companies have cut roads into previously undisturbed forests and removed stands of trees, destroying bonobo nests.

Infrastructure projects like this one in the Congo rainforest may threaten wildlife — and not primarily during construction. New roads and rail lines, even when intended only to facilitate the transport of goods from one point to another, often encourage human settlement and development all along the route.

## COMPETITION FOR LAND

When wild animals and humans live close together, they compete for use of the same land. Local farmers may shoot, trap, or poison wild animals such as lions, hyenas, and leopards to prevent them from preying on their livestock. Villagers might kill elephants, gorillas, and other herbivores that venture into fields of crops in search of food.

Some researchers believe that the population of many large predators has declined because of conflicts with farmers over livestock. One study reported that the 200,000 lions on the continent in the 1980s had been reduced to 20,000 as a result of sport hunting and competition with local farmers. Male lions tend to have large territories, with a range of about 400 square miles (1,000 sq km), which makes it more likely the predators will end up in areas where people live. The lions have been caught between the needs of the human population and their own needs for space and prey.

Fear for their safety also motivates many farmers to try to kill off carnivorous predators in their area. However, plant-eating mammals can present significant dangers as well. A large elephant may eat as much as 440 pounds (200 kg) of vegetation each day, and these massive beasts can easily devastate a farmer's crops. During the breeding season, destructive males (called rogue elephants) have been known to rampage through villages. At a conference convened by South African National Parks in November 2004, one villager explained how people who encounter elephants every day see the world's largest land animals: "They destroy our crops, occupy our drinking places, compete with our livestock for food, and are a danger to our people."

## BUSHMEAT TRADE

Before the 1990s the hunting of wild animals for food, or bushmeat, was practiced mainly by local people such as the Ba'aka of the Congo rainforest. Using traditional snares and traps, they killed only as much as they needed to survive.

During the 1990s, however, logging companies from America, Europe, and Asia began cutting roads into the deep forests of the Congo Basin. In doing so, they opened up new trails and routes for hunters using modern guns to kill deer, forest antelopes, wild pigs, and monkeys, as well as endangered species such as chimpanzees, gorillas, and forest elephants. Some hunters were hired to provide bushmeat for the logging companies' workforces. Others found profits in supplying towns and cities, where bushmeat commands high prices as a delicacy.

In a 2003 BBC report, chimpanzee researcher and conservationist Dr. Jane Goodall described the bushmeat trade:

Hunters from the towns can use the logging trucks to go along the roads . . . they shoot everything from elephants down to gorillas, chimpanzees, bonobos, monkeys, birds—everything.

They smoke it, they load it on to the trucks and take it into the cities, where it's not to feed starving people—it's where people will pay more for bushmeat than for domesticated meat.

Smoked bushmeat continues to be sold in local village markets in the Congo Basin, and it is transported even further away. There is great demand for bushmeat in central, western, and northern Africa, as well as in the Middle East and European cities with large African immigrant communities. As a result, in a relatively short period of time, bushmeat hunting has become a huge commercial business.

Uncontrolled hunting now takes place from the Democratic Republic of the Congo to Cameroon to Nigeria. Although all the countries in these areas have laws to protect wildlife, they are seldom enforced. In Ghana, poachers have reduced the numbers of the black and white colubus monkey, elephant, hippopotamus, and bongo antelope. The eastern region of the Central African Republic has lost 95 percent of its elephant, giraffe, crocodile, and lion populations from its forests and savannas because of the bushmeat trade.

The billion-dollar bushmeat industry is decimating the wildlife of the Congo Basin. In 2002 the Wildlife Conservation Society reported that more than a million metric tons of bushmeat (equivalent to 4 million cattle) was being taken from the Congo forests every year.

One species feared close to extinction is the bonobo, or pygmy chimpanzee, which lives only in the Congo. In a survey of the Democratic Republic of the Congo's Salonga National Park, researchers from the WWF reported that the wild bonobo population had declined from 50,000 to 10,000. At about 90,000 square miles (233,000 sq km), Salonga is Africa's largest protected area

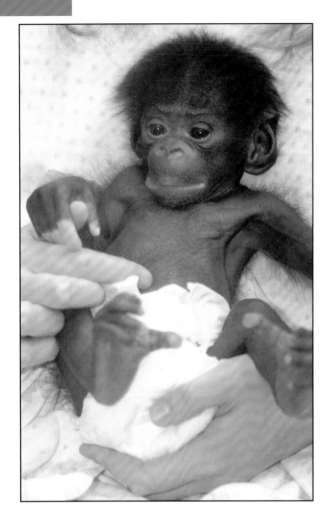

In 2002, when this bonobo (named Vijay) was born at the Cincinnati Zoo and Botanical Garden, there were 141 of the animals—commonly known as pygmy chimpanzees—in captivity worldwide. In the wild, bonobos are found only in a section of the Democratic Republic of the Congo and are endangered.

of tropical rainforest, yet on approximately one-third of the park's land the WWF researchers could find no evidence of bonobos at all. Because of the bushmeat trade, Dr. Goodall warns, Africa's great apes—chimpanzees, bonobos, and gorillas—may go extinct in the wild within the next 15 years. Even great apes in protected areas, such as national parks and wildlife preserves, may be lost as well.

## WILDLIFE TRADE

Some of Africa's wild animals are captured alive to be sold as pets or to zoos and research institutions. Poachers usually want young animals and will kill the mother in order to take a baby. Entire families of gorillas, which live in close-knit groups, may be killed so a hunter can capture one baby gorilla.

Hunters also kill wildlife for body parts. Sometimes gorilla heads or hands are sold locally to tourists as souvenirs. However, poachers get much more money selling animal parts (especially elephant tusks and rhino horns) on the international market.

# ELEPHANT IVORY

Since the 1800s elephants have been hunted as big game trophies and for their tusks of ivory. Both the male and female African elephants have tusks, which are actually elongated teeth. Tusks can grow up to 7 inches (18 centimeters) per year. The largest ones can weigh as much as 160 pounds (73 kg) and reach 12 feet (3.7 meters) long.

During the early 1900s, ivory was sought for making many items, including piano keys, billiard balls, and door handles. Although plastic has replaced ivory in these and other household products today, ivory remains a valuable article of trade. There is a particularly strong market in Asia, where buyers consider carved items made of ivory as status symbols.

Researchers estimate that in 1930 anywhere from 5 million to 10 million elephants roamed the entire African continent. However, habitat loss and hunting decimated their numbers, and today most elephants live south of the Sahara Desert.

Zoologists recognize three species of African elephants, two named after their respective habitats—the savanna elephant (found in sub-Saharan eastern and central Africa) and the forest elephant (found in central and western Africa's rainforests). A third, newly described species called the west African elephant is believed to also live in the rainforests of central, and possibly western, Africa.

Intensive hunting of the African elephant, mostly to feed the ivory trade, took place through much of the 20th century. In 1989 ivory was priced at $100 a pound, and only about 600,000 African elephants remained in the wild. At that time, an international ban was placed on the ivory trade, which caused ivory prices—and the rate of elephant poaching—to fall. In the late 1990s, however, the illegal ivory market grew stronger, and poaching began to increase once more.

Elephant poaching was rampant before the 1989 enactment of an international ban on the ivory trade. Since then, elephant populations have recovered in certain southern African countries, and some of these countries now want to reintroduce limited hunting in order to cull their overly large herds, fund conservation projects, and help local communities.

Some experts estimate that, as a result of continued poaching and habitat loss, African elephants today number only about 300,000. But accurate estimates of wildlife populations can be difficult to determine. A 2003 study by the World Conservation Union estimated that there could be as many as 400,000 to 660,000 elephants on the continent, with the largest numbers in southern Africa.

# RHINO HORN

Because its horn is coveted in the Middle East and Asia, the rhinoceros has seen its population decimated. Many Asians use rhino horn as a traditional medicine for the treatment of ailments such as fever, delirium, and high blood pressure. In Yemen, located opposite the Horn of Africa on the Arabian Peninsula, the trade in rhino horn has been banned since 1982. However, rhino horn is still sold illegally and carved into an elaborate handle for a ceremonial dagger called a *jambiya*, which is a status symbol for its owner.

During the 1970s, about 17,600 pounds (8,000 kilograms) of rhino horn was traded worldwide per year, but the amount dropped in the 1980s to an estimated 6,600 pounds (3,000 kg). In the mid-1990s one pound (.45 kg) of rhino horn sold for as much as $27,000. Because of its high value on the black market, rhino horn continues to be sought by poachers who threaten the animal's very survival.

There are two species of rhinoceros living in Africa: the black rhino and the white rhino. The white rhino is actually not white; its name comes from the Dutch/Afrikaans word *wijdlip*, meaning "wide lip," which was mistakenly translated as "white." Although the white rhino was brought close to extinction at the beginning of the 20th century, today its numbers exceed 11,000. Almost all are members of the same subspecies (southern white rhino); they live mostly in South Africa but can also be found in Botswana and Namibia.

A black rhinoceros roams the Sweetwater's Game Reserve in Kenya. By 2005 poaching had reduced the black rhino's numbers to an estimated 3,600. Rhino horn, used in Yemen to make handles for ceremonial daggers and in Asia for traditional medicines, may fetch more than $25,000 per pound on the black market.

The black rhino has not been so lucky. Its population, which numbered around 1 million at the turn of the 20th century, had been reduced by about 90 percent by 1960. Each decade thereafter, the black rhino population continued in a steady decline. In 1970 an estimated 65,000 could be found throughout sub-Saharan Africa. But by 1980 poaching and habitat destruction had reduced their numbers to 14,000, and they no longer existed in many parts of their former range, including Chad, Ethiopia, Angola, Mozambique, Somalia, and Sudan. As of early 2005, only an estimated 3,600 black rhinos remained.

# DISEASE

Human activities are not the only threat to Africa's animals. Several diseases have also had a severe impact on certain wildlife populations. One of the worst is Ebola hemorrhagic fever. The disease takes its name from the Ebola River in the Democratic Republic of the Congo, where the first recorded case in humans occurred in 1976. Caused by a virus, Ebola can produce massive bleeding; it is fatal 50 to 90 percent of the time. In addition to humans, Ebola affects gorillas and chimpanzees.

In surveys conducted from 1998 to 2000 in Gabon and the Republic of the Congo, researchers found that an epidemic of Ebola hemorrhagic fever had contributed to a steep decline in ape populations in the region. In fact, their numbers had been halved since the last primate census, taken in 1983. The area is believed to contain 80 percent of the world's gorillas (including the western lowland gorilla, the most numerous and widespread of the four subspecies) and most of the world's chimpanzees.

Although bushmeat hunting contributed heavily to the loss of apes and chimpanzees, the researchers believed that the virus had killed thousands, and possibly tens of thousands, of primates. Some areas in the survey had seen a 99 percent decline in ape density. Because there are no known treatments for the disease in humans or primates, the epidemic can only be left to run its course.

Another disease that affects primates, and that is related to Ebola, is Marburg hemorrhagic fever. An outbreak in Angola that began in late 2004 had claimed the lives of more than 250 people by May of the following year. Scientists believe that the disease spreads from infected great apes to humans by means of the bushmeat trade.

But infectious diseases carried by humans also spread to gorillas and chimps living nearby. Some great apes have fallen victim to measles, polio, and tuberculosis.

Livestock also carry diseases that infect wildlife. The cattle disease rinderpest has killed off both wild and domestic herds in Africa. Scientists believe that livestock carried anthrax spores that killed chimpanzees in the Tai National Park, in Côte

**Like humans, animals are susceptible to devastating diseases. This elephant died only 20 minutes after drinking water infected with anthrax bacteria.**

d'Ivoire. Anthrax outbreaks have also killed several hippos in parks and wildlife reserves in Uganda, although park wardens made use of anti-anthrax vaccines to keep the remaining hippos safe.

# INVASIVE ALIEN SPECIES

Yet another threat to native African species has been the intentional or accidental introduction of non-native species—including microorganisms, plants, and animals—that compete with or prey on native species. Because introduced species come from different ecosystems, they often have no natural enemies that would keep their numbers in check.

One of the most serious invaders in Africa is the South American water hyacinth. Brought to Africa as an ornamental plant, it has taken over many of the continent's lakes and rivers. The plant reproduces quickly, doubling in mass in 12 days, and forming huge mats that can cover the surface of the water over thousands of acres.

These mats now choke most of Africa's waterways and have destroyed fish habitats by preventing light and oxygen from reaching beneath the surface of the water. Oxygen levels in the water fall so low that other aquatic plants and hundreds of native fish species have been killed. The Great Lakes area has been particularly hard hit by the water hyacinth, with severe consequences for water supplies, shipping, and hydroelectric power plants (which harness water power from dammed rivers).

Another alien species in the Great Lakes region is the Nile perch, a fish that was introduced to Lake Victoria around the 1960s. It has flourished at the expense of more than 200 native fish species, preying on the other fish and reproducing rapidly.

In South Africa, conservationists are concerned about the effect of invasive species on the Cape floral kingdom. Earth contains only six floral kingdoms, which are defined as regions

**Invasive species have wreaked havoc on parts of Africa. Shown here is a section of the Congo River that has been overrun by water hyacinth, a species native to Brazil that was brought to Africa as an ornamental plant. It has choked many African lakes and waterways.**

containing very high numbers of endemic botanical species. About 80 percent of the vegetation in the Cape floral kingdom consists of *fynbos* (Afrikaans for "fine bush") species. Although the name refers to the fine leaves found on these small shrubs, some of the more than 7,000 different fynbos species have broad leaves. Almost two-thirds of fynbos species are found only in the Cape floral kingdom.

Encompassing a mountainous region of some 35,000 square miles (90,000 sq km) at Africa's southern tip, the Cape floral kingdom contains remarkable botanical diversity. It is home to more than 8,500 plant species, about 5,800 of which are found only in this region. But approximately 1,400 of these species have been identified as critically endangered or close to extinction.

Today, the fynbos is threatened by invading tree species, including the *Hakea* (or needlebush) from Australia, and pine, originally from Europe. These invasive plants have changed the ecosystem so that wildfires occur more frequently and are more intense, which kills the indigenous species' seeds while stimulating the germination of those of invading species.

Many other alien species have invaded Africa's environment. In 2003 the World Conservation Union issued a report on invasive species in Africa's wetlands (freshwater ecosystems such as swamps, springs, rivers, and lakes that depend on freshwater flows for existence). The study found that the damage from alien species in Africa's waterways was costing the continent $400 billion per year.

# PROTECTING AFRICA'S BIODIVERSITY

I n recent times Africa has seen a dramatic decline in its biodiversity. The major causes of this decline in the variety of plant and animal species found on the continent include hunting, poaching, and the illegal wildlife trade, as well as habitat loss from desertification, deforestation, and the pressures of an increasing human population. In order to protect endangered species and their habitats, African nations have passed various laws and signed international treaties. They have set aside land for preserves and national parks. And they have tried to educate people about the importance of biodiversity.

## LAWS AND TREATIES TO PROTECT VULNERABLE SPECIES

Most African countries have laws to protect vulnerable species. However, in areas of great poverty and civil unrest, wildlife protection laws tend to be ineffective, poorly enforced, or undermined by local corruption. In some cases, officials in charge of stopping illegal hunting are actually involved in poaching rings themselves. And when poachers are caught, they typically receive small fines and light punishment.

Billions of dollars change hands every year among those who trade in wild plants and animals (living or dead) and their body parts and products. To protect vulnerable species from extinction, more than 160 countries around the world have signed on to the Convention on International Trade in Endangered Species of Wild Fauna and Flora, or CITES (pronounced SITE-ease). This conservation treaty, which is administered by the United Nations, came into force in 1975 with the purpose of regulating international trade in species identified as threatened or endangered.

CITES has identified more than 30,000 endangered and threatened species of animals and plants in the world today. They are categorized according to the degree of protection needed. Appendix I identifies about 1,000 plant and animal species that are threatened with extinction; commercial trade in these species is banned. African species in Appendix I include great apes (mountain and lowland gorillas, bonobos, and chimpanzees), leopards, cheetahs, the African elephant (except the populations of Botswana, Namibia, South Africa, and Zimbabwe), Grevy's zebra, and the black rhino. Appendix II lists species that, while not immediately threatened with extinction, may become so if trade is not closely regulated; limited trade and sales are allowed if special permits are issued. Among the approximately 4,100 animal species and 28,000 plant species native to Africa that are listed in Appendix II are the common and pygmy hippopotamus, the southern white rhinoceros, various chameleons of Madagascar, the emperor scorpion, and the marsh rose and Swartland sugarbush (two plants found in South Africa). Appendix III designation has

In 2004 game farmer John Hume (above) stood in support of South Africa's decision to ask the Convention on International Trade in Endangered Species for the right to sell 10 black rhino hunting licenses per year. South Africa consistently has one of the most successful conservation programs on the continent. The hunts would help keep the herd to a sustainable size and fund further conservation efforts.

been assigned to approximately 300 species that are protected in at least one country.

CITES members meet every two and a half years to reevaluate the Appendix classifications and make adjustments to trade regulations. Member countries are required to follow rules in monitoring, regulating, and even eliminating trade in specified species. The private conservation organizations WWF and the World Conservation Union work with CITES and with central and local governments to help ensure that protective bans are enforced.

# REGULATING THE IVORY TRADE

Within the 10-year period from 1979 to 1989, the African elephant population dropped by 50 percent, from an estimated 1.3 million to 600,000. East Africa was hardest hit, as numbers in

Kenya declined by 80 percent, and in Uganda and Sudan by 90 percent. In response, CITES established a ban on the ivory trade by adding the African elephant to Appendix I in 1989. However, several southern African countries had large elephant populations, and they lobbied for the right to sell the ivory, as well as skins and meat, of animals from their herds.

In response, CITES allowed Botswana, Namibia, and Zimbabwe to sell ivory to Japan in 1999, and in 2002 Botswana, Namibia, and South Africa were given permission to sell ivory to Asian markets. Critics complained that such sales would raise the price of ivory and attract more poaching, since it is not possible to tell whether ivory has been obtained from legal sources. Many conservationists feared that poaching would increase because a market for ivory had been reinstituted.

In the late 19th and early 20th centuries, ivory from the African colonies was so plentiful in Europe that it was used to make standard utilitarian items such as this grooming kit.

Such fears appear to have been well founded, as studies show that elephant poaching is again on the rise. In 2005 a study funded by Care for the Wild International reported that poachers were killing 6,000 to 12,000 elephants per year. The places most affected were southern Sudan, the Democratic Republic of the Congo, the Central African Republic, Chad, and Kenya. According to the report, poachers were transporting the ivory for sale on the black market in Sudan's major cities of Khartoum and Omdurman. There, it was being bought and shipped to Asia by Chinese workers for Sudan's oil, mining, and construction industries.

TRAFFIC (the investigative arm of the WWF and IUCN) released a report in 2003 censuring the West African countries of Côte d'Ivoire, Senegal, and Nigeria for allowing the ivory trade to flourish. Because anti-poaching laws have not been enforced, the elephant populations in western and central Africa are seriously threatened. Some conservation groups have even accused Sudan's government of supporting the ivory trade and of allowing its military to provide security and transportation to poachers carrying ivory back from central Africa.

## PROTECTING THE RHINO

South Africa contains almost 90 percent of the world's white rhinos. This subspecies, known as the southern white rhino, is so plentiful that it was transferred to Appendix II of CITES in 1994. This means that the government of South Africa can sell the animal to zoos and wildlife preserves, and even allow a limited number to be hunted for sport trophies, as long as the proper permits are in place.

All other rhino species and subspecies appear on Appendix I of CITES because they are considered in danger of extinction. However, the black rhino's numbers have shown some improvement recently, rising from a low of 2,400 in 1995 to 3,600 in

2004. These gains, according to the World Conservation Union's African Rhino Specialist Group, can be attributed to several factors. First, the four countries that contain the majority of the black rhino population (South Africa, Namibia, Kenya, and Zimbabwe) have instituted more effective anti-poaching measures. These include beefed-up patrols in parks and reserves, better training and equipment for security personnel, and increased legal penalties for poachers (typically prison sentences of 5 to 10 years). Captive breeding programs run by government organizations and conservation groups have also helped increase the black rhino population.

Critically endangered rhino subspecies include the northwestern black rhino (found only in Cameroon) and the northern white rhino (found only in the Democratic Republic of the Congo). In parks where rhino numbers have dropped to just a few, extreme measures may be taken to protect them. In some parks and reserves they may be kept under continuous armed guard, while in their habitat during the day and while locked up at night. Sometimes park wardens de-horn the animals so poachers have no reason to kill them.

## PREVENTING THE BUSHMEAT TRADE

Conservation groups are calling on governments to pass and enforce laws to reduce the impact of the bushmeat trade. Among the proposed laws are bans on the transport of bushmeat over long distances and limitations per region on the number of people allowed to hunt wildlife, with the trade restricted to species that are not in danger of becoming extinct. Some environmentalists believe that further development of Africa's domestic livestock and fishing industries would also reduce the killing of wildlife by providing alternative sources of protein, such as beef, chicken, and fish.

# ALTERNATIVES TO KILLING PREDATORS

The continuing loss of Africa's wild predators could also be prevented, some conservationist groups believe, by educating farmers about alternatives to poisoning, trapping, and killing animals that prey on livestock. For example, to reduce the number of wild lions being killed in Kenya, the Kilimanjaro Lion Conservation Project has provided game scouts to teach anti-predator management of livestock. One technique promotes the use of traditional enclosures, or *bomas*, for keeping cattle, goats, or sheep safe at night. Other methods include using experienced adults instead of children to herd livestock, and keeping dogs to warn of predators.

The Cheetah Conservation Fund, headquartered in Namibia, promotes the use of a specific breed of dog for guarding livestock. The organization, which is working to prevent the extinction of wild cheetahs in southern Africa, notes that typical herding dogs try to move animals to safety when they spot danger, and such actions cause the cheetah to respond instinctually by stalking and chasing. Instead of herding dogs, the Cheetah Conservation Fund provides farmers with guard dogs—specifically, Anatolian shepherds. This large, powerful breed—which can weigh up to 150 pounds (68 kg)—will challenge all kinds of predators, including cheetahs, jackals, lynx, leopards, and baboons, by standing its ground and barking. The Livestock Guarding Dog Program of the Cheetah Conservation Fund, along with related educational programs, has met with success in reducing the number of big cats being shot and killed in Namibia (from 800 to 900 per year in the 1980s to around 200 per year today).

# PROMOTING ECOTOURISM

Economic considerations (protecting farms and livestock or selling animal products such as ivory, rhino horn, and bushmeat)

**The Namibia-based Cheetah Conservation Fund has provided farmers with Anatolian shepherds. The powerful dogs deter attacks on livestock, reducing the need for farmers to kill cheetahs in order to protect their herds.**

provide strong motivation for some people to kill Africa's wild animals. But keeping wildlife alive can also provide economic benefits. And, as some conservationists and governments have recognized, the key to preserving Africa's biodiversity may lie in ecotourism—promoting wildlife and natural habitats as tourist attractions.

Ecotourism has pumped millions of dollars annually into the economies of several African countries. Nature lovers from around the world journey to Africa to view its unique animals in their natural habitat. Especially popular are the "Big Five"—the lion, leopard, elephant, rhino, and buffalo—but tourists are also drawn by such animals as the cheetah, giraffe, and hippo, along with various antelopes and bird species.

Ecotourism brings tangible economic benefits to local people. It creates jobs as rangers and trackers, cameramen, managers, guides, and teachers. Related businesses in the hospitality industry (campgrounds, safari lodges, hotels, and restaurants) employ local people as well. Even the sale of locally made crafts by roadside vendors can be sustained by a strong tourist economy.

Ecotourism has proven particularly valuable in Kenya, where government officials estimate that 8 out of 10 visitors to the country come for the wildlife. The tourist industry has also strengthened the economy in South Africa, which has seen its number of visitors rise significantly over the past decade.

# VALUE OF ECOTOURISM IN PROTECTING ENDANGERED SPECIES

Ecotourism has been credited with helping the mountain gorilla of East Africa survive. Native to the Virunga forests, which border the Democratic Republic of the Congo, Rwanda, and Uganda, the mountain gorilla has for some time been in danger of becoming extinct because of poaching. Indeed, one of the people who brought the gorilla's plight to the world's attention was American zoologist Dian Fossey, who was herself murdered by poachers.

In 1979 the Rwandan government and a consortium of conservation groups (the WWF, African Wildlife Foundation, and Fauna & Flora International) established the Mountain Gorilla Project. This conservation program provided tourists with limited visits to see the gorilla families, but at high admission charges of $170 a day. The money paid for local guides' salaries and for habitat preservation. Because tourist fees made the gorillas worth more alive than dead, poaching decreased. In the years that followed, Rwanda became well known for its gorillas, and tourism ranked as the country's third-largest source of foreign income.

In 1989 a census survey indicated that there were 324 mountain gorillas living in the Virunga forests. However, beginning in

1990, wars in Rwanda and later in the Democratic Republic of the Congo made further population counts impossible. It was late 2003 before the wars ended and the region became secure enough to take a new census of the gorillas.

Despite fears that the mountain gorilla population would have been decimated by the conflicts and by poaching, the 2003 census actually revealed an increase in the numbers. Conservationists believe the gorilla population grew to 380 because the local people recognized the gorillas' value to them and had a stake in their welfare. Although some gorillas had been lost to poachers, eco-tourism had helped the endangered mountain gorilla population increase by 17 percent in a region decimated by war.

## NATIONAL PARKS AND NATURE PRESERVES AND PARKS

Africa has over 1,200 national parks, wildlife reserves, and other protected areas covering more than 772,000 square miles (2 million sq km). These areas, as well as private parks (located primarily in Kenya and South Africa), provide a basis for the tourist industry and related livelihoods for millions of people, particularly the rural poor.

Hunting in these protected areas is supposed to be outlawed or controlled. In many cases, however, a lack of financial resources or inadequate policing leaves the lands underprotected.

Inadequate protection may bring the northern white rhino to extinction in its last known wilderness habitat, the Garamba National Park. Located in the northeastern corner of the Democratic Republic of the Congo, Garamba lies along the border with Sudan. One of the oldest national parks in Africa (established in 1938), Garamba contains a natural grassland ecosystem that is home to thousands of elephants and buffalos, the last of the Congo giraffes (fewer than 100), and the northern white rhino. The most threatened rhinoceros subspecies in the

Ecotourism is a major source of income for nations such as Kenya and South Africa, and its potential economic benefits have been touted in other wildlife-rich African countries as well. Modern safari-goers travel in vans with modified pop-up tops, and they shoot animals with cameras rather than guns.

world, the northern white rhino has been exterminated in all of its former habitats of central Africa.

Commercial poaching between 1978 and 1984 reduced the number of northern white rhinos in Garamba from 490 to 15. Concerned about the animal's possible extinction, park managers and conservation groups helped increase the rhino population to 30 by the year 2000. But in mid-2003, Sudanese militiamen entered the park, using military weapons to hunt bushmeat for commercial markets and poach ivory and rhino horns. Garamba park guards lacked the equipment and other resources to prevent the intrusions.

In August 2005 only 4 northern white rhinos were believed to remain in the wild, although 10 were in captivity. Despite appeals by numerous conservation groups, the president of the

Democratic Republic of the Congo refused to allow the emergency translocation of the rhinos to a wildlife sanctuary in Kenya. However, in October 2005, government officials agreed to allow the African Parks Foundation to assume management of the park—providing a boost in financial resources to protect it.

Intense poaching has also had a severe impact in East Africa's parks, including Kenya's largest national park, Tsavo East. Covering about 4,700 square miles (12,000 sq km) of southeastern Kenya, Tsavo East National Park is home to an estimated 800,000 animals, including zebras, dik-diks (a small antelope), rhinos, lions, leopards, and elephants, all of which forage on the dry grasslands. The park, like many others in Kenya, supports a lucrative tourist industry.

A study published in 2004 estimated that since 2001, some 300,000 of Tsavo East's animals had been lost to poachers annually because of the bushmeat, rhino horn, and ivory trades. In fact, the study reported, since 1990 poaching had caused wildlife throughout Kenya to decrease by as much as 60 percent.

## TOO MANY ANIMALS

By contrast, South Africa has seen an increase in the populations of many of its wildlife species. In particular, the elephant population has exploded, according to managers of Kruger National Park, which holds 90 percent of South Africa's elephants and is the country's largest and oldest park. More than 340 species of trees, 115 species of reptiles, and 500 species of birds, as well as 150 mammal species, reside within the park. Long considered a model for nature conservation, Kruger National Park was entirely fenced until 1994, and it was adequately staffed to prevent poaching. As a result, its wildlife population has grown rapidly.

In order to keep the elephant population in check, between the 1960s and the mid-1990s, park managers allowed adult elephants to be killed and the young exported. Hides and meat were sold in the international market, and meat was canned for domestic use. However, the 1989 CITES ban cut off the international trade, and in 1995, in response to conservationists' protests, the park stopped culling its elephant herds.

Now the park's 7,800 square miles (20,000 sq km) cannot support its burgeoning elephant population, which increased from fewer than 7,000 in 1995 to about 13,000 by 2004. Food has become scarce; elephants have stripped the park of its vegetation and begun ravaging crops of adjacent farms. Competition for food has also led elephants to attack other species, including the endangered black rhinoceros.

A pair of game wardens on the lookout for poachers. Unfortunately, those charged with protecting wildlife in Africa's national parks and game reserves often find themselves outnumbered and outgunned by well-organized gangs of poachers.

Other countries in southern Africa also have large elephant populations. In northern Botswana, approximately 120,000 elephants roam land large enough to sustain only about 50,000. The impact on habitat in Botswana's Chobe Reserve and the wetlands wilderness of the Okavango Delta has been severe.

One way of dealing with elephant overpopulation, administrators at Kruger National Park have found, is to relocate some animals to underpopulated reserves. However, this practice is time-consuming and costly, requiring that the animals be tranquilized and airlifted to their new home. Several animals must be transferred at a time, because elephants are socially oriented creatures and have the best chance of survival when moved with their family groups. Kruger park managers have also been considering reinstituting the practice of killing elephants to reduce their numbers.

**Large, social, and highly intelligent, elephants are a favorite of animal lovers throughout the world. But in southern Africa, successful conservation programs have led to an explosion in elephant populations, forcing park managers to confront difficult choices.**

# TRANSFRONTIER CONSERVATION AREAS

Another possible way to deal with overpopulation of species such as the elephant is to establish transfrontier parks and corridors between parks. These measures would allow elephants to follow their old migration routes to lands that have space for them.

The first protected region allowing wildlife to cross unfenced national borders came into existence in 2000, when the Kgalagadi Transfrontier Park united the Gemsbok National Park in Botswana with the Kalahari Gemsbok National Park in South Africa. This semi-desert protected area is run as a single unit, and as a transfrontier park, it allows wildlife (including the gemsbok, springbok, and Kalahari lion) to migrate freely between the nations of Botswana and South Africa.

Transfrontier conservation areas are commonly referred to as peace parks, because they exist through the efforts of people and governments working together to manage the land and the animals living there. The removal of fences between borders allows animals to gain access to water. Open parks particularly help elephant and lion populations, which commonly range or migrate over hundreds of miles.

Another peace park is the Okavango/Upper Zambezi Transfrontier Park, which straddles five countries—Namibia, Botswana, Zimbabwe, Angola, and Zambia. The development of this cross-border reserve has included UN funding to help Angola clear landmines from ancient elephant migratory routes. At least 2,200 landmine sites have been identified, the result of almost 30 years of civil war in Angola. It is hoped that the removal of the explosives will lure Botswana's elephants across the borders. Even though they live in overcrowded circumstances, the elephants have not migrated into Angola and Zambia, some scientists believe, because the animals sense danger from the explosives in the ground.

In December 2002, the heads of state of Mozambique, South Africa, and Zimbabwe signed a treaty that paved the way for the establishment of the Great Limpopo Transfrontier Park. At about 13,500 square miles (35,000 sq km), this peace park is larger than New Jersey and Connecticut combined. But its creation was only the first stage in an ambitious plan to establish a huge transfrontier conservation area covering some 38,600 square miles (100,000 sq km).

# LOCAL OWNERSHIP OF RESOURCES

Educating people to manage wildlife responsibly is difficult in impoverished regions. The very poor, concerned with simply surviving from day to day, may not consider the long-term consequences of overexploiting natural resources. However, government efforts to preserve wildlife can lead to problems.

Unfortunately, central governments in Africa have too often set up national parks and nature preserves without regard for the people living in and around those regions. Once the paperwork establishing parkland is signed, activities that local people have long used to support themselves, such as hunting, may become illegal. Thus they may be unable to continue their traditional way of life.

For example, villagers living within the eastern Mantadia forest reserve of Madagascar do not understand why they are banned from clearing the rainforest for agricultural use. They do not see their actions as destructive to biodiversity because of habitat loss, but as the only way to make a living. A chief elder explained his confusion in a 2005 BBC news report: "Our village has been burning forests to plant rice here for generations. Then suddenly they come and tell us we no longer have the right to do this. This is our way of life. If we can't cut the forests, we can't feed ourselves."

New conservation initiatives have taken the approach that local communities should be empowered to decide how wildlife in their regions is managed. Referred to as Community-Based Natural Resource Management, this practice calls for giving local people the legal rights to wildlife, with the understanding that they will manage it in a sustainable manner.

Such community-owned areas were established in remote regions of northwestern Namibia in the 1980s, and the move brought an end to severe poaching. Following independence from South Africa in 1990, the new Namibian government allowed the permanent establishment of official bodies, or conservancies, in which the local people held legal rights to the wildlife. Dozens of such conservancies exist today in Namibia, generating income that is used to provide funding for the health, education, and transportation needs of the local people, while keeping wildlife alive and well for future generations.

# ENVIRONMENTAL POLLUTION

Over the last half century, as Africa's population has increased, so too has the amount of pollution in the environment. The most serious problems have resulted from the development and use of fossil fuels (coal, oil, and natural gas) for energy and from the improper disposal of waste.

## COMMERCIAL ENERGY USE IN AFRICA

Of all the world's inhabited continents, Africa uses the least amount of energy. Most people have a low standard of living and are too poor to own cars, household appliances, or other energy-consuming items that are commonplace in industrialized nations. In fact, only a relatively small percentage of the African population has access to electricity, and national power grids—where they exist—are frequently plagued by maintenance and service problems.

South Africa produces the largest amount of electricity of all countries of Africa. Electrical power comes mostly from coal-fired plants, but also from the continent's only nuclear power reactor and some hydroelectric plants. The majority of South Africa's residents are connected to its national power grid. In fact, South Africa generates enough electrical power to export electricity to the neighboring countries of Lesotho, Swaziland, Namibia, Botswana, Zimbabwe, and Mozambique, which are all linked on a vast grid. (South Africa also imports electricity generated by the Cahora Bassa Dam, Mozambique's hydroelectric facility along the Zambezi River.)

Egypt has the second-largest installed electricity capacity on the continent. Most of the country's electrical power comes from natural-gas-fired generators; the rest is supplied by hydroelectric power, produced mainly by the Aswan Dam. Though it is plagued by frequent power outages, Nigeria also has a large number of electricity-generating plants (natural gas as well as hydroelectric).

However, the people in many other African countries do not have access to any national power grids at all. In Ethiopia, only 14 percent of the population is connected to such a network. Uganda has even fewer citizens with electricity, although its government has set a goal to serve 10 percent of its population by 2012.

## DEPENDENCE ON FOSSIL FUELS

Many African countries have tapped into their deposits and reservoirs of coal, oil, and natural gas to help fuel their economies. Algeria and Egypt produce and export natural gas. The North Africa region also supports crude oil production, particularly in Egypt, Algeria, and Libya, all of which export primarily to Europe.

Oil production has driven the economies of several sub-Saharan countries as well. The largest oil producers of sub-Saharan Africa, according to 2004 estimates, were (in descending order) Nigeria, Angola, Gabon, Equatorial Guinea, Sudan, the Republic of the Congo, Chad, and Cameroon.

South Africa and Botswana produce almost all of Africa's coal, which is both used domestically and exported. The countries in the eastern region of Africa produce almost no oil, coal, or natural gas and must import these fuels from other countries.

# AIR, SOIL, AND WATER POLLUTION FROM COAL

Fossil fuel production and use harms the environment. When coal is mined, chemicals contaminate the water beneath the earth's surface, or groundwater, with toxins. When burned as fuel, coal releases into the atmosphere ash and particulates (tiny particles of liquid or solid matter), as well as gases such as sulfur dioxide and nitrogen dioxide. When these gases react with water vapor, they form sulfuric and nitric acid in the air, and subsequent precipitation falls as acid rain. Because it raises the acidity in lakes, acid rain can kill fish and other aquatic life. It can also devastate vegetation and forests.

**A worker delivers a bag of coal to a customer in Soweto, South Africa. When coal is burned to heat homes or to fire electrical power plants, acid rain can result.**

The largest producer and user of coal in Africa, South Africa depends on this fossil fuel for more than 90 percent of its electricity generation. The technology to remove sulfur from coal-burning power stations exists, but thus far this technology has not been widely used in South Africa because of its expense.

Unlike most of its sub-Saharan neighbors, South Africa has a strong industrial economy, producing cars, chemicals, textiles and clothing, processed foods, and iron and steel. However, many of its industrial centers, such as the Vaal Triangle and Milnerton, in Cape Town, have significant "hotspots" of air pollution.

# AIR, SOIL, AND WATER POLLUTION FROM OIL AND NATURAL GAS

Pollution in oil-producing countries of Africa has degraded the air, ground, and water. During the oil-extraction process, large amounts of natural gas are produced. Most oil-producing companies have their workers burn off this gas, in a process known as gas flaring. The practice releases huge amounts of carbon dioxide into the atmosphere. Not only does gas flaring pollute the air, but it also wastes a potentially valuable resource—natural gas. The World Bank, an organization that funds many programs in developing nations, has estimated that the amount of natural gas lost in Africa each day is equivalent to 12 times the energy that the continent uses on a daily basis.

Oil development has also degraded the land and water in many oil-producing countries of Africa. Oil spills, leaks, and accidents occur along pipelines and shipping ports because of poor maintenance and lax regulations. The viscous, toxic liquid has destroyed marine life and wildlife habitats such as seabeds, wetlands, and marshes.

One area particularly degraded by oil production and a lack of environmental regulations is the Niger Delta, a lagoon and mangrove swampland that contains large oil deposits. For decades, spills from oil installations have been common: according to a report by the Energy Information Administration (EIA) of the U.S. Department of Energy, more than 4,000 spills have occurred in the Niger Delta since 1960. Oil toxicity has had a profound effect on the indigenous people of the area: their water is no longer drinkable. Their mangrove forests, which provided them with fuelwood, have been killed. And, by some estimates, each oil spill has caused the deaths of hundreds of thousands of fish and other marine life that the people depend on for food and their livelihoods.

Spills also occur when thieves puncture pipelines with drills and hacksaws so they can siphon off fuel for sale on the black market. Such spills sometimes cause explosions, deadly fires, and severe environmental damage to farmland and streams. In October 1998 one fire engulfed approximately 2,000 men, women, and children who were scooping up gasoline with cans and buckets from a punctured pipeline. More than 1,000 died.

Other African countries whose coastal waters have been polluted by oil wastes include Egypt, Algeria, Morocco, Liberia, and

An oil spill burns in Goi, Nigeria. Petroleum production has had severe environmental consequences in Nigeria, the world's eighth-largest exporter of crude oil, particularly in the country's Niger Delta region.

South Africa. Although South Africa does not contain oil deposits, it is home to several refineries, and a high volume of tanker traffic plies the waters off its coast en route from the oil-rich Middle East to Europe and the United States. In June 2003 a significant tanker spill off the coast of Cape Town threatened the South African penguin population.

# AIR POLLUTION FROM INDUSTRIALIZATION AND URBANIZATION

Africa currently has a faster rate of urbanization than any other region of the world, and it is becoming increasingly industrialized. These trends promise to create an ever-greater need for power, along with rising emissions of harmful gases, as governments scramble to provide the electricity needed to run factories, businesses, and homes, typically without the benefit of pollution-reducing technologies.

Already, air pollution is a concern in many of the big cities of Africa, where streets are often congested with old, inefficient cars and trucks that run on high-polluting leaded gasoline and lack emissions control technology. Few African countries have placed restrictions on vehicle emissions.

The 1.2 million vehicles on the streets of Cairo have been blamed for the heavy smog that hangs over Egypt's capital city, which is also packed with 15 million people. Particulates from industry and vehicle emissions hang in the air, mingling with sand particles blown from the neighboring Western Desert. Africa's second-largest city, Lagos, Nigeria, is also blanketed by smog caused, in part, by its high density of trucks and automobiles as well as the gas flaring practices of local oil industries. Further pollution results when residents turn to diesel generators for electricity during the frequent power outages that plague Lagos.

Smog hangs over Cairo, one of the world's most congested—and polluted—cities. The World Health Organization reports that residents of Egypt's capital are subject to 20 times the level of acceptable air pollution.

In sub-Saharan Africa, 70 percent of energy used in both rural and urban locations comes from the burning of wood and charcoal, a practice that adds large amounts of particulates to the air. People also burn agricultural debris and animal waste as fuel. The use of dirty fuels in cooking stoves in poorly ventilated homes has been linked to respiratory illnesses and other health problems.

# SOIL AND WATER POLLUTION FROM INDUSTRIALIZATION AND URBANIZATION

Africa's mining industry has also done great damage to its environment. Degradation has been most severe in coal-producing regions of South Africa and in the Democratic Republic of the

Congo, which produces coltan (a metallic ore that is refined into a product used in capacitors for computers, cell phones, and other electronic devices), diamonds, and gold. Other nations that have suffered significant environmental damage from mining include Guinea and Zimbabwe. Poor mining practices have led to pollution from poisonous wastes and heavy metals (toxic metals such as mercury and lead), as well as soil erosion.

In urban areas, the waste products of industrial processes have polluted rivers, lakes, oceans, and groundwater. Industry effluents have contaminated the waterways of Côte d'Ivoire and Lake Victoria, which is shared by Kenya, Tanzania, and Uganda. Oil and chemical spills have destroyed water basin habitats and killed birds, fish, and other wildlife in Nigeria and Zambia. Industrial solid wastes, such as poisonous chemicals and heavy metals, placed in open dumps and landfills have contaminated Cairo's groundwater and the Nile River.

Tanzania's national environment agency has warned that the country's water supply is being poisoned from untreated industrial waste pumped into the country's rivers. Analysis of one industrial region in Dar es Salaam showed that the water contained high levels of toxic metals such as mercury and lead.

The most heavily populated areas of Africa suffer from the most severe soil and water pollution. Much of it comes from human waste. Inadequate city sanitation systems allow sewage to spill untreated into rivers and lakes—and eventually to make its way to oceans. According to the United Nations Environment Program (UNEP), 107 million people along the coasts of western and central Africa are at risk of disease and death because their drinking water has been contaminated by untreated sewage. The UNEP reports that 19 million Africans living along Africa's eastern coast are similarly affected. Water that has been polluted with human waste carries bacteria that can cause illnesses such as cholera and dysentery.

A health worker in Tanzania treats a child for trachoma. Caused by a bacterium that is often present in contaminated water, trachoma is responsible for more cases of preventable blindness worldwide than any other cause. The majority of its victims live in sub-Saharan Africa.

# WATER POLLUTION FROM AGRICULTURAL USE

Deforestation and soil erosion also contribute to water pollution because they cause topsoil to run off into rivers. Sediment runoff may cloud the water, which blocks light from aquatic plants, eventually killing them. Sometimes runoff adds nutrients to the water, stimulating algae growth that decreases the amount of oxygen in the water. This process, called eutrophication, can also kill off many aquatic plants and animals.

Sediment and nutrient runoff have been blamed for the explosive growth of the South American water hyacinth infesting Lake Victoria. Since the 1960s, as much as 3.2 million tons of fertile soil has been washed downstream from western Kenya into Lake Victoria. The nutrients from this sediment have fostered the water hyacinth's mat-like growth so that it has covered the lake, which in turn has lowered the oxygen level in the water enough to kill off hundreds of native fish species.

Coastal waters have also been polluted when sediment from land that has been treated with fertilizers and pesticides washes downstream to the oceans. Fertilizer and agricultural runoff are particularly serous environmental problems in Algeria and South Africa.

# REGULATING ENVIRONMENTAL POLLUTION

Many African governments have passed legislation to address their environmental problems. Among the acts and laws passed are the 1991 Ghanaian National Environmental Plan, the 1994 Egyptian Law for the Protection of the Environment, and the 1995 Ugandan National Environmental Statute. Although most countries have few stringent environmental regulations in place to prevent environmental pollution, public outcry has forced some governments and companies to address specific problems.

For example, the Nigerian government has moved to address concerns about gas flaring, which releases huge amounts of carbon dioxide into the atmosphere. By 2008 Nigeria intends to eliminate the practice, requiring oil companies to capture natural gas released in the extraction of petroleum.

Some African countries with oil-refining industries are moving to comply with restrictions imposed by other countries, such as the United States and Western European nations, that have agreed to buy their diesel fuel and gasoline. In Angola, refineries are being built to meet specific technical and environmental requirements.

Legislators in South Africa are developing laws to address the country's air pollution problems. Among the new legislation is a mandatory changeover from leaded to unleaded gasoline. The new diesel and gasoline motor fuels will contain less sulfur as well. When these fuels are burned, they will emit lower levels of lead and sulfur into the atmosphere.

As a child, the man in this photo—who is from the Nigerian fishing village of Akaraolu—was burned when petroleum from a nearby oil well ignited. The flare in the background, which burns off the natural gas produced when the oil is extracted, has been lit continuously since 1972, causing a variety of serious health problems for residents of Akaraolu.

# REDUCING POLLUTION USING ALTERNATIVE ENERGY

Building dams to harness water for electricity is seen by some environmentalists as the answer to Africa's need for reliable, clean, and renewable energy. Hydroelectric power plants do not produce the pollutants emitted by electrical power plants dependent on oil, coal, or natural gas for fuel. However, the construction of hydroelectric plants can have a devastating effect on the environment. These dams can flood the habitats of wildlife and the villages of local people, and they can cause freshwater habitats to dry up because of diverted water supplies.

Some countries have turned to cleaner, renewable sources of power such as wind-powered electricity generators. Among African countries making use of "wind farms" to generate electricity are Egypt (in Zafarana) and Tunisia (in Hawariya).

Solar-powered generating units, which use the sun to charge solar cells for electricity, are another potential clean-energy source. Solar energy could prove especially useful in remote rural areas, where it would be expensive to connect people to national electricity grids. Zambia, Namibia, and South Africa have been evaluating the feasibility of providing such off-grid electrification to some of their citizens.

Some countries have taken steps to promote solar energy development. Zambia has eliminated import duties on solar panels, Namibia has helped establish a solar module factory in the country, and Mauritius is planning to use solar-powered street lamps in its capital city.

## CLEANING WASTEWATER

Wetlands naturally absorb and filter out harmful pollutants, purifying water. Efforts to keep Africa's ponds, reed beds, and mangrove swamps healthy and intact could solve sewerage problems in many rapidly growing cities. Because these ecosystems can serve as inexpensive sewage filtering systems, they need to be kept healthy and intact. That is, they cannot be drained and cleared to make room for homes or for agricultural use.

For example, instead of spending $13 million on construction of a sewerage system, city administrators in Kampala, Uganda, depend on a wetlands area located south of the capital. Preservation of wetlands not only provides for the means for filtering human sewage, it also maintains wildlife habitats for birds, fish, and other animals.

In an effort to cleanse water on the Nairobi River, the Nairobi River Basin Initiative (funded by the United Nations Environment Program) plans to convert a dam into an artificial wetland, with reed beds and plants. The region is currently a sea of green, clogged with mats of water hyacinth and polluted with rubbish, raw sewage, and waste from manufacturing and food processing industries. Although the water would not be suitable for drinking, it should be clean enough for use in industry and irrigation for the city of Nairobi, which currently uses drinking water for these activities.

The World Agroforestry Centre (ICRAF) is working to help clean up severely polluted waters in Kenya with programs that will introduce bamboo along Lake Victoria and the riverbanks of its tributaries. It is hoped that the bamboo, which absorbs water faster than most plants and soaks up toxins, will help clean the region's waterways and in effect provide wastewater treatment for some municipalities. Although bamboo forests once grew in most of Kenya's water catchments, most were cleared so the land could be planted with sugarcane and coffee.

In Namibia, high-tech solutions have been applied to the problem of cleaning wastewater—with excellent results. Windhoek, the capital, boasts a state-of-the-art system by which municipal sewage is treated, filtered, and then recycled for household use (including drinking). Half of the water used in the city of 160,000 residents is fully recycled.

<br>**WATER SHORTAGES**

**A**ccess to safe drinking water is a severe problem facing the entire world. According to the World Health Organization, almost one-sixth of the world's population lacks access to potable water. In other words, approximately 1.2 billion people do not have water that is safe to drink. The World Resources Institute predicts that by 2025, at least 3.5 billion people will face serious water shortages.

The need for clean, safe water is particularly pressing in Africa. Because of drought, desertification, and pollution, many people cannot find potable water. In some parts of the continent, fewer than 50 percent of the people have access to safe, clean water.

## WHAT CAUSES WATER SHORTAGES?

Although water covers 75 percent of the earth's surface, 97.5 percent of it is saltwater. Of the remaining 2.5 percent that is freshwater, most is either frozen in polar ice caps and glaciers or is in underground aquifers. Humans have easy access to only a small fraction of the earth's freshwater, from rivers and lakes.

The amount of freshwater in the world is unevenly distributed. Some parts of the world have much more freshwater than others. The Middle East, North Africa, and parts of western and central North America are particularly dry. In Africa, water is most scarce in the Sahara Desert and Sahel region to the north, and the Namib and Kalahari Deserts to the south. However, the continent has abundant freshwater resources in its large rivers, such as the Congo, Nile, and Zambezi, and in its Great Lakes region.

The world's population has more than doubled since the 1950s, from 2.5 billion people in 1953 to over 6 billion people today. And by 2050, experts predict, the world's population will have reached 8.9 billion.

The growing population is creating an increasing demand on the freshwater needed for human use, agriculture, and industry—despite the fact that the amount of available water in the environment remains the same. Currently most freshwater is used not for drinking, but for agriculture and industry. According to the UN's World Water Assessment Program, 70 percent of freshwater used goes to agriculture, 22 percent to industry, and 8 percent to domestic use (drinking, washing, cooking, and sanitation). According to the UN, the minimum amount of water people need for domestic use is 50 liters (about 13.2 gallons) per day.

In some parts of the world, freshwater has been contaminated by human and industrial wastes. More than 12 million people die every year from drinking this unsafe water, which often carries bacteria or other organisms that cause diseases such as cholera, dysentery, schistosomiasis, filariasis, and trachoma.

Waterborne diseases are currently a major cause of death, particularly in poor areas of the world. According to the World

Health Organization, illnesses caused by unclean water and poor sanitation kill about 4,000 children every day. In sub-Saharan Africa, 43 percent of children drink unsafe water—and one in five never reach their fifth birthday.

# WATER SCARCITY IN AFRICA

Researchers for the Global Water Policy Project in Africa estimate that water scarcity affects some 300 million Africans (about 38 percent of the population). Water shortages claim at least 6,000 lives per year.

Fourteen countries, most in northern Africa, have been identified as currently affected by water stress (defined as each person having access to less than 1,500 cubic meters of water per year) or water scarcity (access to less than 1,000 cubic meters per person annually). Those numbers are likely to become even worse. The United Nations Development Program predicts that by 2025, half of all Africans will be living in countries with water stress or water scarcity.

The likelihood of future water shortages will prevent developing nations in Africa from guaranteeing a steady food supply, since farmers without access to water cannot raise crops or livestock. Water shortages in Africa have led to severe famines in the past and threaten to do so in the future.

# LOSS OF WATER BECAUSE OF WETLANDS DEGRADATION

Less water in Africa is being purified by wetlands because many of these water ecosystems have disappeared, claimed by humans for development or agriculture, or dried up by dam construction. Other wetlands have been overwhelmed by flourishing invasive species and severe pollution.

Officials in southwestern Uganda predict that parts of the region will run out of water by 2010 because of the draining of

A poor continent, Africa is sorely in need of development, but projects that strip the land of vegetation can have a negative impact on the supply of clean water.

lands for agricultural use. The waterways and lakes of East Africa's Great Lakes region hold water unfit for human use because of the water hyacinth infestation and pollution from raw sewage, chemicals, and heavy metals. Numerous oil spills have contaminated the drinking water in parts of the Niger River Basin.

Efforts are under way to make local people aware of the dangers of drinking water that may be contaminated with sewage or tainted by industrial waste. Among the long-term health problems associated with waters polluted by heavy metals are cancer, poisoning, and skin disease. Despite education efforts, however, many poor people will use whatever water they can find because they have no other options; they cannot afford to buy water, and free sources of clean water are not available where they live.

## WATER WASTE IN AGRICULTURE

Agriculture consumes the bulk (70 percent) of the freshwater used by people, and most of it goes to irrigation. About 6 percent of Africa's farmland is irrigated, according to a 2004 Global Water Policy Project report. Although this is much less than the world average of 18 percent, Africa's irrigation practices have been extensive enough to contribute to desertification in the Sahel. In West Africa, large-scale irrigation systems have lost unused water to the desert.

The usual methods of irrigating land—with ditches, flooding, or sprinkling—can waste most of the water being used. Studies have shown that as much as 60 percent of water extracted for irrigation never reaches the roots of crops. The UN Food and Agriculture Organization (FAO) has estimated that as much as 90 percent of water used for farming in arid countries is wasted, mostly because of evaporation and irrigation seepage.

## ACCESS TO WATER IN RURAL AREAS

The lack of water helps keep rural Africans in poverty, since so much of their time must be spent walking to rivers or ponds to fetch water. African women are usually tasked with this job. They walk an average of six miles (9.7 km) to a water source, and then they must carry the heavy container back, usually balanced on the head. Sometimes the chore of hauling water falls to children. The time spent searching for and bringing back water, some point out, could be better spent for adults in working or growing crops and for children in attending school.

Governments and nongovernmental organizations have provided rural villagers with water by drilling boreholes and digging wells that access underground aquifers. Public workers and charity groups have also helped villagers dig out ponds that fill during rainy seasons and help keep aquifer levels high. Obtaining water from underground supplies has its risks because if too many boreholes are drilled in an area, the groundwater in that region can be used up and the water table will fall.

## ACCESS TO WATER IN THE CITIES

As Africa's cities have grown, greater strains have been placed on their often antiquated water-service infrastructures, such as pumps and pipes. Corruption in and poor management of water-service companies is frequent, and even city residents who are well-off enough to have water taps in their homes cannot be assured of a steady supply. In Ghana, the water service in many cities is so bad that most people have water tanks they can fill during the infrequent times that the taps do run. The poorest people in cities tend not to have

A woman in Senegal demonstrates the hand-cranked water pump that was installed in her town. Many towns and villages in Africa do not have any running water, so people must walk to natural sources, such as rivers, which are often several miles away.

service and must pay high prices for buckets of water sold by private vendors.

However, in some cases, water service is reliable and far-reaching. A determined effort by the South African government has ensured that the majority of the country's residents have drinking water. In 1994, when the African National Congress came to power, 12 million out of South Africa's 38 million people did not have access to clean water. By 2002 those numbers had greatly improved: only 7 million of the 42 million people did not have access. (South Africa defines access as piped water in cities and in villages, with "a working standpipe within 200 meters of every home.")

The first 6,000 liters (1,585 gallons) per month of water is free; consumers must pay for whatever amount they use beyond that. For a family of four, 6,000 liters per month averages out to 50 liters (13.2 gallons) per person per day, which is the bare minimum of water recommended by the United Nations. The South African government has set the goal of providing everyone in the nation with water by 2008.

## POSSIBLE WATER WARS

As Africa's population grows, and more agricultural and economic development takes place, the demand for water will increase. The possibility exists that dwindling water resources could lead to conflicts over water rights.

For example, approximately 160 million people from 10 different countries live in the Nile Basin. However, Egypt and Sudan claim the rights to determine how other nations can use the waters of the Nile, based on a 1929 treaty (revised in 1959) between Egypt and Great Britain. The agreement requires countries south of Egypt to get its approval for any irrigation or hydroelectric projects on the Nile or its tributaries. Egypt has no other freshwater sources except the Nile, and an Egyptian official once said that the country was prepared to use force to protect its rights to the river.

Several nations believe the treaty needs to be revised to provide equitable use for all 10 nations in the Nile Basin. Tanzania and Kenya wish to use Lake Victoria (which feeds the Nile) for drinking water and irrigation projects. The issue is being addressed by the Nile Basin Initiative, a partnership established in 1999 to promote sustainable development and management in the region.

Other areas that share major river systems in Africa are the Niger River Basin in West Africa (which supports 10 million people in nine countries), and the Okavango system in southwest Africa, which Botswana and Namibia share. More than two-thirds of Africa's 60 river basins are shared by more than one country, and rivers serve as boundaries for many others.

# WATER DEVELOPMENT PROJECTS

Many African governments have invested in the construction of large dams. Such projects are often built to provide electricity, as well as to create water reservoirs for growing urban populations, irrigate farmland, and prevent seasonal flooding.

However, the building of massive dams has been shown to create many other environmental problems. People are displaced and forestlands are flooded by dam reservoirs, while downstream wetlands and their natural filtering systems for sewage and other pollutants are lost. Dams disrupt the volume, timing, and quality of water flows, disturbing the migration, breeding, and feeding of freshwater species downstream.

Some environmental activists have worked to halt the construction of dams by placing pressure on funding organizations such as the World Bank. However, many African government officials see such structures as the only feasible way to provide water for their people.

Dams tend to have a limited lifespan because they block silt carried by river, and the buildup of sedimentation eventually fills the reservoir. Normally, this silt would have been carried downstream to the river's lower basin, providing fertile soil to that area. For example, Egypt's Aswan Dam, built in 1968, has provided hydroelectric power and water for irrigation, but it has also blocked the Nile River from depositing fertile soil in the delta. This sedimentation remains trapped in Lake Nasser, forcing Egyptian farmers to use artificial fertilizers on their soil instead.

In Ghana the Akosombo Dam, when built in the 1960s, created one of the world's largest man-made lakes, Lake Volta. In the process, however, the project displaced 80,000 people. The lake has since caused serious health problems for people living in the area, such as an increase in sleeping sickness and malaria.

Environmental activists believe that the negative impact of dams on the environment and the local people is too great. To address issues of water scarcity, they favor educating people to

**A satellite photo of the Aswan Dam. Although it has provided much-needed hydroelectric power to Egypt, the Aswan Dam prevents the annual flooding of the Nile River, reducing the fertility of the land in the Nile Delta region.**

conserve water and use it responsibly at all times, not just during droughts. Environmentalists point out that governments can also conserve water by preserving natural systems such as forests and wetlands.

Libya plans a project described as the largest water development scheme in the world. To address the country's limited natural freshwater resources, the North African country is constructing the Great Manmade River Project, which is designed to bring water from aquifers under the Sahara Desert to the country's coastal regions. Libya hopes the project will provide water for irrigation and supply water to its major cities.

# REDUCING THE IMPACT OF DAMS

Environmentalist groups such as the WWF point out that it is possible to lessen the impact of dams on wetlands by arranging for the release of water flows that can revitalize freshwater ecosystems. The organization has made an agreement with the government of Zambia and its national electricity company that should bring life back to the Kafue Flats wetlands in Zambia, which has been declining because of two dams controlling water flow through the region.

The irregular water flow (released intermittently for electricity generation) has affected the area's two national parks, as well as the livelihoods of local people dependent on the region's fisheries and commercial sugar plantations. According to the agreement, the electricity company will use a more natural flooding schedule, which should allow for the conservation of the wetlands system while still providing power for Zambia's people.

# REDUCING WATER WASTE IN AGRICULTURE

Environmentalists recommend that greater efforts be made in Africa to conserve the large amounts of water being lost unnecessarily to agriculture. Such conservation efforts already exist in some parts of the continent.

For example, in South Africa and Swaziland, some farmers routinely "harvest" rainwater. In South Africa, they collect it in storage tanks located in fields and use it for drinking water and irrigation. Swaziland farmers collect rainwater from barrels placed beneath roof overhangs or concrete containers at the end of gutter pipes.

Because rainfall in Swaziland has decreased significantly in the past few years, the government has passed laws regulating the amount of water a resident can take from a river or stream. Farmers are limited to the amount needed to irrigate "one-quarter hectare" (a little more than half an acre) of land. Certain rivers, such as the Ngwavuma River in southern Swaziland, are off-limits entirely because unregulated industries have polluted them with toxins. The government forbids residents to use water from these rivers, recommending instead that they use boreholes and streams.

Many new technologies that are not affordable or widely available could help African farmers decrease the huge amount of water currently lost in agricultural practices. Drip irrigation systems and low-pressure sprinklers would prevent evaporation that occurs when water is sprayed. The development of drought-resistant crops would also greatly reduce the amount of water used in agriculture. For example, it now takes a ton (nearly 300 gallons) of water to produce just 2.2 pounds (1 kg) of wheat, according to the UN Food and Agriculture Organization.

## MAKING PROGRESS

In 2004 the UN reported that between 1990 and 2002, 1.1 billion more people had access to clean water. In fact, 83 percent of the world had safe water to drink, compared with only 77 percent in 1990.

Some countries in Africa have improved significantly in this regard. For example, Angola, which was at war for most of the UN study period, still managed to provide 50 percent of its people with safe water by 2004, up from about 33 percent in 1990.

Others still need much more help. Around 70 percent of Tanzania's rural population has no access to protected water sources. And more than 70 percent of the population in Nigeria is plagued by water scarcity. Although the Nigerian government has initiated many water supply projects over the years, water shortages persist across the country. In Ethiopia 75 percent of the people do not have safe water to drink, and 85 percent do not have benefit of sewage systems. Not surprisingly, perhaps, most of the illnesses treated in Ethiopia result from water-related diseases.

# MILLENNIUM DEVELOPMENT GOALS

In September 2000 the United Nations adopted eight Millennium Development Goals, which UN member states have pledged to meet by 2015. These include "Eradicate extreme poverty and hunger," "Achieve universal primary education," "Combat HIV/AIDS, malaria and other diseases," and "Ensure environmental sustainability." Under this last category is the target of cutting in half the proportion of people in the world without sustainable access to clean water. How to accomplish this remains to be determined, as not everyone agrees on the best solutions. Infrastructure projects such as dams and water pipelines compete with calls for better conservation measures. However, the UN does believe that emphasis must be placed on educating people about the importance of water and the need to conserve and develop water resources.

# CLIMATE CHANGE

Over the past 140 years, scientists have recorded distinct changes in the world's climate. In some parts of the world, temperatures are higher than usual. In other regions, previously warm areas have become significantly cooler. Rainfall in some areas has increased, while drought has taken over in others. Africa has proven extremely vulnerable to these changes. An increase in the number of severe floods and droughts during the past few decades has cost the lives of hundreds of thousands of people and animals.

## WHAT IS CLIMATE CHANGE?

Most of the earth's atmosphere consists of nitrogen (78 percent) and oxygen (21 percent). Although present in very small amounts, other gases also play a critical role in maintaining the conditions necessary to sustain life on earth. They include carbon dioxide, methane, and nitrous oxide, which form a layer in the atmos-

(Opposite) Sun sets on the Masai Mara Game Reserve in Kenya. In the coming years, some experts predict, Africa's fragile ecosystems will be particularly vulnerable to climate change.

phere that keeps earth's climate warm by preventing heat energy from the sun from radiating back into space. The process by which heat is trapped near earth's surface is known as the "greenhouse effect," and carbon dioxide, methane, and nitrous oxide are often referred to as "greenhouse gases."

While earth would be uninhabitable without the greenhouse effect, there is broad agreement among scientists that human activity is producing increasing levels of greenhouse gases in the atmosphere and, consequently, a rise in global temperatures. Many scientists worry that global warming might cause—or might already have begun causing—profound climatic changes.

These changes include shifts in wind and rain patterns (making some regions drier and others wetter), along with an increase in "extreme climate events" (such as disastrous storms, droughts, or floods) in some parts of the world. Climate change, in turn, might dramatically alter ecosystems, threatening many animal and plant species with extinction.

# WHY ARE GREENHOUSE GASES INCREASING?

Many human activities have been blamed for causing the increase in greenhouse gases. The burning of fossil fuels such as coal, oil, and natural gas emits large amounts of carbon dioxide and methane into the atmosphere. Even the raising of cattle and cultivation of rice releases methane and nitrous oxide.

Environmentalists generally point to industrialized nations as the source of most carbon dioxide emissions. These countries burn the greatest amounts of coal, oil, and gas because their inhabitants depend on fossil fuels for transportation, manufacturing, heating, cooling, and electrical power. Scientists have shown that levels of carbon dioxide in the atmosphere have risen by a third since the 1760s—when the industrial revolution began in Europe.

Deforestation also contributes to increased carbon dioxide in the atmosphere. Of particular concern has been the ongoing loss of earth's rainforests. Rainforests absorb huge amounts of carbon dioxide from the atmosphere and convert it into oxygen. When trees are cut down, the forests can take in less carbon dioxide, so the gas builds up in the atmosphere. The Amazon rainforest in South America and the Congo rainforest in Africa have been referred to as the world's lungs, essential for maintaining a livable climate. The rapid destruction of these forests has been identified as a significant factor in the increased levels of carbon dioxide in the atmosphere.

# POSSIBLE SIGNS OF CLIMATE CHANGE IN AFRICA

A 2002 UNEP report noted that since 1968, rainfall has been decreasing in parts of Africa. The continent has seen numerous major droughts since the late 1960s—in the Sahel region from 1968 to 1974, in Ethiopia in the early 1980s, and in parts of southern Africa in the early 1990s. Some scientists believe that droughts have become more common in Botswana, Burkina Faso, Chad, Ethiopia, Kenya, Mauritania, and Mozambique because of climate change. Others argue that recent droughts are attributable to natural climate variations. Whatever the case, the impact on human life has been severe, with drought conditions causing crop failures that, in turn, lead to food shortages and famines.

**Shifting wind and rain patterns have the potential to devastate parts of Africa, a continent that is already prone to droughts. Unfortunately, droughts in Africa almost inevitably produce food shortages and famine. This photo was taken in 2002, in the midst of a food shortage in Zimbabwe.**

But changes in weather patterns have also caused devastating floods in Africa. In 1997 parts of East Africa suffered extreme flooding. Somalia saw the heaviest rains in half a century, and the resulting floods killed at least 1,600 people and washed away whole villages, forcing 250,000 people to flee their homes. That same year, Uganda, Kenya, and Ethiopia experienced heavy flooding as well, and hundreds of thousands of people lost their homes, livestock herds, and crops to the deluge.

# GREENHOUSE GAS EMISSIONS FROM AFRICA

In 2002 the UNEP reported that carbon dioxide emissions in Africa had increased eightfold since 1950. However, all the countries in Africa combined still produce less carbon dioxide emissions than the United States (or China) alone. (Four countries—South Africa, Egypt, Nigeria, and Algeria—account for more than three-quarters of the continent's total carbon dioxide emissions.)

Nevertheless, the burning of fuelwood and overall forest depletion in Africa has contributed to the increase in greenhouse gases in the atmosphere. And activities such as slash-and-burn agriculture, in which Africa's arid and semiarid grasslands have been periodically burned, also emit greenhouse gases. A 2003 report stated that fires set by farmers to clear land for crops were partially to blame for a highly visible sign of climate change: the rapid melting of the ice cap atop Mount Kilimanjaro.

# CONVENTION ON CLIMATE CHANGE AND THE KYOTO PROTOCOL

At the 1992 Earth Summit held in Rio de Janeiro, world governments recognized climate change as a problem by signing on to the United Nations Framework Convention on Climate Change.

The treaty stated that greenhouse gas concentrations in the atmosphere needed to be stabilized at a level "sufficient to allow ecosystems to adapt naturally to climate change, to ensure that food production is not threatened and to enable economic development to proceed in a sustainable manner."

Nations that eventually ratified, or legally accepted, the treaty continued to meet annually to determine ways to accomplish the goal of stabilizing greenhouse gases. At the December 1997 meeting, in Kyoto, Japan, 39 countries signed an agreement in which they promised to meet specific targets to curb greenhouse gas emissions. This agreement, referred to as the Kyoto Protocol, ultimately called for industrialized nations to cut, by the year 2012, their collective emissions of carbon dioxide and other greenhouse gases to 5 percent below 1990 emission levels.

The Kyoto Protocol came into force on February 16, 2005, after it had been ratified by 141 countries. Among the major nations that had not ratified the protocol were the United States (the world's largest emitter of greenhouse gases) and Australia.

All sub-Saharan nations except for Somalia and Liberia have signed and ratified the UN Framework Convention on Climate Change. As developing countries, however, they do not need to reduce their greenhouse gas emissions at this time.

# GLOSSARY

**ACID RAIN:** rainfall that is acidic (because of high levels of sulfuric acid and nitric acid, caused by air pollution).

**BIODIVERSITY:** biological diversity; variety that exists among different types of animals and plants.

**BUSHMEAT:** wildlife killed for food.

**CLIMATE CHANGE:** broadly, any change in long-term climatic trends (such as changes in average temperature or average precipitation), regardless of the cause; according to the definition used by the United Nations Framework Convention on Climate Change, "a change of climate which is attributed directly or indirectly to human activity that alters the composition of the global atmosphere and which is in addition to natural climate variability observed over comparable time periods."

**DEFORESTATION:** the act of removing trees from forests, or the clearing of trees from land.

**DESERTIFICATION:** the process by which viable land is turned into dry land that cannot support plant life.

**DEVELOPING NATION:** a country with low per capita income.

**ECOSYSTEM:** an interrelated network of living and non-living things in a particular area; habitat.

**ECOTOURISM:** recreational travel to natural habitats, typically in a manner designed to have minimal impact on the environment.

**ENDANGERED SPECIES:** species identified as threatened with extinction.

**ENDEMIC:** found naturally in only one place in the world.

**GAS FLARING:** the process by which natural gas is burned off during the extraction of petroleum; considered environmentally damaging because it releases carbon dioxide into the atmosphere.

**GLOBAL WARMING:** an increase in temperatures at the earth's surface, believed to be caused by a buildup of greenhouse gases in the atmosphere and to be the cause of climate change.

**HABITAT:** the place where an animal or plant naturally lives or grows.

**INDIGENOUS:** native to an area.

**POACHING:** illegal hunting.

**RAINFOREST:** a woodland area that has an annual rainfall of at least 100 inches (254 centimeters).

**RENEWABLE RESOURCES:** resources that can be replaced with time through natural processes.

**SAVANNA:** a large, grassy plain with only scattered trees.

**SUSTAINABLE USE:** the use of renewable resources at a rate that allows their ongoing replacement.

**WETLANDS:** freshwater ecosystems such as swamps, springs, rivers, and lakes.

# FURTHER READING

Buchanan, Molly. *Safari: The Romance and the Reality.* Washington, D.C.: National Geographic, 2003.

Long, Douglas. *Global Warming.* New York: Facts On File, 2004.

Morris, Patrick. *Wild Africa: Exploring the African Habitats.* New York: DK Publishing, 2002.

Reader, John. *Africa: A Biography of the Continent.* New York: Alfred A. Knopf, 1998.

Shah, Anup, and Manoj Shah. *The Circle of Life: Wildlife on the African Savannah.* New York: Harry N. Abrams, 2003.

# INTERNET RESOURCES

**HTTP://WWW.CLIMATEHOTMAP.ORG/AFRICA.HTML**

Detailed information on the impact of global warming in Africa. Includes a map indicating various locations where climate change has been evident.

**HTTP://WWW.REDLIST.ORG**

Compiled by the World Conservation Union (also known as the International Union for the Conservation of Nature and Natural Resources), this list of species considered critically endangered, endangered, or vulnerable is updated yearly.

**HTTP://WWW.NATIONALGEOGRAPHIC.COM/AFRICA/**

Contains links to various stories on Africa by *National Geographic* magazine, as well as resources to links for maps, travel information, and news.

**HTTP://WWW.ICRAFSA.ORG**

This organization is dedicated to improving the lives of the agricultural poor, while also sustaining the global environment. The website describes some of its innovative programs in Malawi, Mozambique, Tanzania, Zambia, and Zimbabwe.

**HTTP://WWW.PANDA.ORG**

Operating in more than 100 countries, WWF funds projects to help solve environmental problems around the world. Follow the link to Africa for specific information on efforts in individual African nations.

# FOR MORE INFORMATION

## UNITED NATIONS ENVIRONMENT PROGRAM (UNEP)

United Nations Ave., Gigiri
P.O. Box 30552, Nairobi, Kenya
Phone: + 254 20 623074 / 624161
Fax: + 254 20 623741
http://www.unep.org

## WORLD CONSERVATION UNION (INTERNATIONAL UNION FOR THE CONSERVATION OF NATURE AND NATURAL RESOURCES)

IUCN Headquarters
Rue Mauverney 28
1196 Gland
Switzerland
Phone: + 41 (22) 999-0000
Fax: + 41 (22) 999-0002
E-mail: mail@iucn.org
http://www.iucn.org

## WWF INTERNATIONAL

Avenue du Mont Blanc
CH 1196 Gland
Switzerland
Phone: + 41 22 364 9111
http://www.panda.org

# INDEX

Numbers in **bold italic** refer to captions.

INDEX

# PICTURE CREDITS

# CONTRIBUTORS

**PROFESSOR ROBERT I. ROTBERG** is Director of the Program on Intrastate Conflict and Conflict Resolution at the Kennedy School, Harvard University, and President of the World Peace Foundation. He is the author of a number of books and articles on Africa, including *A Political History of Tropical Africa* and *Ending Autocracy, Enabling Democracy: The Tribulations of Southern Africa*.

**LEEANNE GELLETLY** is a freelance writer and editor living outside Philadelphia. She is a graduate of Muhlenberg College, in Allentown, Pennsylvania, and has attended classes at New York University, in New York, and at the Great Valley campus of Penn State University, in Malvern, Pennsylvania. Ms. Gelletly has worked in publishing for more than 20 years and has written on a variety of subjects. Her books include the biographies *Harriet Beecher Stowe* and *Mae Jemison*; geography titles that explore Bolivia, Colombia, Somalia, and Turkey; and discussions of social issues such as Mexican immigration in the United States and violence in the media.